Agenda-Setting

COMMUNICATION CONCEPTS

This series reviews enduring concepts that have guided scholarly inquiry in communication, including their intellectual evolution and their uses in current research. Each book is designed as organized background reading for those who intend further study of the subject.

COMMUNICATION CONCEPTS 6

Agenda-Setting

James W. Dearing
Everett M. Rogers

SAGE Publications
International Educational and Professional Publisher
Thousand Oaks   London   New Delhi

For information address:

 SAGE Publications, Inc.
2455 Teller Road
Thousand Oaks, California 91320
E-mail: order@sagepub.com

SAGE Publications Ltd.
6 Bonhill Street
London EC2A 4PU
United Kingdom

SAGE Publications India Pvt. Ltd.
M-32 Market
Greater Kailash I
New Delhi 110 048 India

Printed in the United States of America

Library of Congress

ISBN 0-7619-0562-6 (c)   ISBN 0-7619-0563-4 (p)

ISSN 1057-7440

96 97 98 99 10 9 8 7 6 5 4 3 2 1

Sage Production Editor: Michèle Lingre

Citation instructions:
When citing a Communication Concepts issue, please follow this reference style:

Dearing, James W., & Rogers, Everett M. (1992), *Communication Concepts 6: Agenda-Setting*. Thousand Oaks, CA: Sage.

Contents

Foreword

Each volume in the Communication Concepts series deals at length with an idea of enduring importance to the study of human communication. Through analysis and interpretation of the scholarly literature, specialists in each area explore the uses to which a major concept has been applied and point to promising directions for future work.

Agenda-setting is that rarity, a scholarly topic that was invented within the field of mass communication research. Both the term itself and a prototypic design for its empirical study date from an original article by Maxwell McCombs and Donald Shaw published in *Public Opinion Quarterly* in 1972. The phrase has become accepted in the popular literature. News analysts today take for granted that we know what they mean when they distinguish the media's agenda-setting power from more direct forms of political persuasion. More important, agenda-setting has proven highly provocative as a research concept, as the lengthy Suggested Readings section of this volume demonstrates.

James Dearing and Everett Rogers have organized this sprawling literature into major categories that, despite sharing a common name, are quite different in their purposes and in the kinds of research suggested. The authors draw a fundamental distinction between studies of the relative priorities among a set of public issues and the life history of a single issue as it competes for a high priority on the agenda. The first type of study was introduced by McCombs and Shaw, scholars with a primary interest in the role of the press in society. The second genre, typified by Rogers and Dearing's own work on public attention to AIDS, is more issue driven and theoretically akin to research on diffusion. This has become the more common approach, adapting the agenda-setting model to the work of mission-oriented agencies such as those dealing with public health problems.

These basic research formats have in turn spawned numerous offshoots, including field experiments on media effects, institutional studies of news judgments, and investigations of the role of public opinion in policy making. Dearing and Rogers provide an organized view of a lively domain of communication research, as illustrated by capsule descriptions of leading studies. We are given a close look at the scientific pursuit of an idea of both practical and theoretical import.

Steven H. Chaffee, *Series Editor*

Preface

We became involved in agenda-setting research in the mid-1980s when we carried out a critical review and synthesis of this topic, presented as a paper at the American Association for Public Opinion Research conference in 1986. We identified three main components in the agenda-setting process: (a) the media agenda, (b) the public agenda, and (c) the policy agenda. This framework was expanded into our 1988 chapter, "Agenda-Setting Research: Where Has It Been? Where Is It Going?" in *Communication Yearbook 11*. This review and critique was cited by half of the agenda-setting publications appearing since 1988 and appears to serve as a useful review for many scholars. This chapter was widely cited because it proposed that agenda-setting is best understood as a process of interaction among three types of agendas.

We then responded to one of our main criticisms of past agenda-setting studies by conducting an over-time study of the agenda-setting process for a single issue: AIDS in the United States (Rogers, Dearing, & Chang, 1991.

We continued our research, writing several articles and chapters about agenda-setting, and then presented invited papers at anniversary sessions of the 1992 American Political Science Association conference and the 1992 American Association for Public Opinion Research conference, celebrating the beginning of agenda research 20 years earlier. Now, both of us are doing new agenda-setting research, from macro-level, cross-national comparisons to micro-level studies of communities and the issues important to them.

We are not founders of agenda-setting research, like communication scholars Max McCombs and Donald Shaw or political scientists Roger Cobb and Charles Elder. We came into this research front during its second decade of empirical investigation and, along with other scholars, helped broaden the research approaches to agenda-setting. We have led in calling for alternative approaches to agenda-setting research, such as the shift from hierarchy studies of the public agenda to longitudinal investigations of one or a few issues. Any scholarly paradigm experiences a successive winnowing of investigative scope as scholars seek to explain and predict particular phenomena. Yet we think that a broader perspective about agenda-setting is most in keeping with the insightful perspectives of the forerunners of agenda-setting research: Walter Lippmann, Robert E. Park, Harold D. Lasswell, Herbert Blumer, Gabriel Almond, Daniel Boorstin, James Davis, E. E. Schattschneider, and Bernard Cohen.

Our students at Michigan State University and at the University of New Mexico are interested in the agenda-setting process as a means of understanding social change. Yet, despite the more than 350 publications about agenda-setting, there is no clear starting place for the student who wants a holistic introduction to this important topic. Here we provide a means to get acquainted with this growing and diverse literature about an exciting scholarly topic that offers explanations of how social change occurs.

Many scholars and students contributed to our perspective on the agenda-setting process, especially Maxwell McCombs, an anonymous reviewer, and the editor of this series, Steven H. Chaffee. We thank our colleagues Soonbum Chang, Dorine Bregman, Xiaoxing Fei, Wen-Ying Liu, and Judy Berkowitz for their help with our agenda-setting research over the past decade.

COMMUNICATION CONCEPTS 6

AGENDA-SETTING

JAMES W. DEARING
EVERETT M. ROGERS

1. What Is Agenda-Setting?

The press may not be successful much of the time in telling people what to think, but it is stunningly successful in telling its readers what to think *about*.

Bernard Cohen (1963, p. 13)

The definition of the alternatives is the supreme instrument of power.

E. E. Schattschneider (1960, p. 68)

Every social system must have an agenda if it is to prioritize the problems facing it, so that it can decide where to start work. Such prioritization is necessary for a community and for a society. The purpose of this book is to help readers understand the agenda-setting process, its conceptual distinctions, and how to carry out agenda-setting research.

Agenda-Setting as a Political Process

What is agenda-setting? The *agenda-setting process* is an ongoing competition among issue proponents to gain the attention of media

1

professionals, the public, and policy elites. Agenda-setting offers an explanation of why information about certain issues, and not other issues, is available to the public in a democracy; how public opinion is shaped; and why certain issues are addressed through policy actions while other issues are not. The study of agenda-setting is the study of social change and of social stability.

What is an agenda, and how is one formed? An *agenda* is a set of issues that are communicated in a hierarchy of importance at a point in time. Political scientists Roger Cobb and Charles Elder (1972/1983) defined an *agenda* in political terms as "a general set of political controversies that will be viewed at any point in time as falling within the range of legitimate concerns meriting the attention of the polity" (p. 14). Although we conceptualize an agenda as existing at a point in time, clearly agendas are the result of a dynamic interplay. As different issues rise and fall in importance over time, agendas provide snapshots of this fluidity.

Cobb and Elder (1972/1983) defined an *issue* as "a conflict between two or more identifiable groups over procedural or substantive matters relating to the distribution of positions or resources" (p. 32). That is, an issue is whatever is in contention (Lang & Lang, 1981). This two-sided nature of an issue is important in understanding why and how an issue climbs up an agenda. The potentially conflictual nature of an issue helps make it newsworthy as proponents and opponents of the issue battle it out in the shared "public arena," which, in modern society, is the mass media. The issues actually studied by agenda-setting scholars and reported in this volume, however, display the two-sided nature claimed by Cobb and Elder (1972/1983) only to a certain degree. For example, the abortion and gun-control issues seem to be definitely two-sided and conflictual. Certain other issues, such as the environment or drug abuse, seem to be more one-sided in that no one takes a public stand in favor of pollution or greater use of drugs. Even for these issues, however, issue opponents do exist who actively campaign for less attention and funding being given to an issue such as cancer prevention so that greater resources can be given to another issue that they are promoting on the national agenda. Yet there is another important aspect of an issue in addition to conflict. There are many social problems that never *become* issues even though proponents and opponents exist. Problems require exposure—coverage in the mass media—before they can be considered "public" issues.

Thus, we define an *issue as a* social problem, often conflictual, that has received mass media coverage. Issues have value because they can be used to political advantage (Ansolabehere & Iyengar, 1994). Although conflict is often what makes a social problem a public issue, as in the case of abortion, *valence issues* only have one legitimate side, such as drug abuse or child abuse (Baumgartner & Jones, 1993; Nelson, 1984). No one is publicly in favor of child abuse. For valence issues, proponents battle over how to solve the agreed-upon social problem and not whether a social problem exists.

The perspective of Cobb and Elder (1972/1983) and Lang and Lang (1981) that an issue is two-sided and involves conflict reminds us that agenda-setting is inherently a political process. At stake is the relative attention given by the media, the public, and policymakers to some issues *and not to others* (Hilgartner & Bosk, 1988). We can think of issues as "rising or falling" on the agenda or "competing with one another" for attention. *Issue proponents,* individuals or groups of people who advocate for attention to be given to an issue, help determine the position of an issue on the agenda, sometimes at the cost of another issue or issues. Agenda-setting can be a "zero-sum game" because space and time on the media agenda are scarce resources (Zhu, 1992a). But sometimes, a hot issue does not supplant coverage of other issues, especially related issues (Hertog, Finnegan, & Kahn, 1994).

An issue proponent might be a newsperson covering a famine in an African nation who shoots a spectacular 3½-minute news story in a refugee camp that is broadcast on U.S. evening television news. Because of the investment of time, effort, and firsthand experience, the reporter becomes a proponent of the famine as an important issue worthy of news attention and public concern. Attention to an issue, whether by media personnel, members of the public, or policymakers, represents power by some individuals or organizations to influence the decision process. The reporter covering the famine may have been influenced to shoot the story from a certain perspective because of discussions with a foreign government official who was frustrated with his or her country's lack of response to the famine. The visual power of the video footage, in turn, may influence an editor's decision about the relative importance of the famine news story in relation to other possible news stories. The news, when broadcast, influences millions of people in a variety of ways. Thousands of television viewers call an 800 telephone number to donate money and food. Some viewers work to change U.S. foreign policy about disaster relief to the African nation. A Senate staff member drafts legislation in the name of her boss. Hundreds of newspaper editors and other media gatekeepers decide that the famine deserves prominent news coverage. Several newspaper readers write letters to the editor to protest U.S. government food aid in the face of poverty in America. Thus, the famine becomes a two-sided issue. Within a few weeks, the very real but little-known famine problem is transformed into the "famine issue" and climbs to the top of the media agenda in the United States. The reporter gets a promotion.

The famine may continue to attract attention or it may not, depending on (a) competition from other issues, each of which has its proponents, and (b) the ability of proponents of the famine issue to generate new information about the famine so as to maintain its newsworthiness. So, whether we study television producers, interest group activists, or actions by U.S. senators, the process of influence, competition, and negotiation *as carried out by issue proponents* is a dynamic driving the agenda-setting process. Most communication scholars have not conceptualized agenda-setting as a political process. A better understanding of the agenda-setting process lies at the intersection of mass communication research and political science. Agenda-setting can directly affect policy.

The issue of cigarette smoking is a dramatic example of the agenda-setting process. Prior to 1970, smoking was a major social problem in America, with millions of people dying of cancer. It was not, however, an important public issue. Then, over the next 25 years, 30 million Americans quit smoking! How did this problem become an issue? The antismoking issue got on public agendas (for instance, citizens groups lobbied for legislation to force the airline industry to ban smoking on all flights), on media agendas (fewer characters, both heroes and villains, now smoke in prime-time television shows), and on policy agendas (the city of Los Angeles pioneered in banning all smoking in restaurants, a policy that spread to other cities). The social norm against smoking became accepted as a result of *media advocacy*, the strategic use of the mass media for advancing a public policy initiative (Wallack, 1990). Issues previously perceived to be the problems of individuals ("I don't like it when people smoke while I am eating") are redefined as a public problem requiring governmental remediation ("Restaurants should be required to offer nonsmoking sections"). Successful media advocacy essentially puts a specific problem, framed in a certain way, on the media agenda. Exposure through the mass media allows a social problem to be transformed into a public issue.

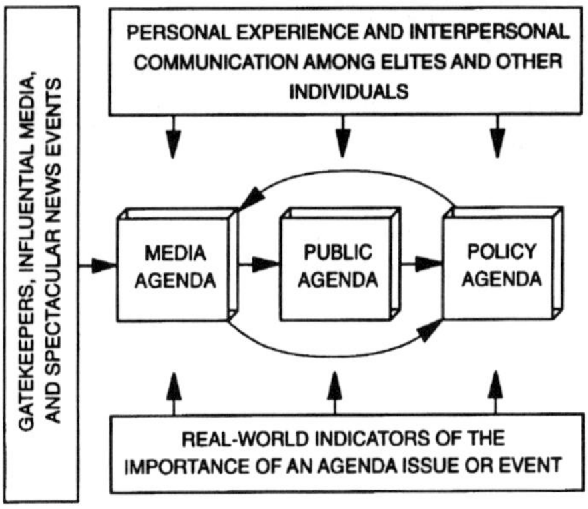

Figure 1.1. Three Main Components of the Agenda-Setting Process: The Media Agenda, Public Agenda, and Policy Agenda
SOURCE: Rogers and Dearing (1988).

Media personalities and organizations engage in issue advocacy. For example, will the aggressive overseas marketing by U.S. cigarette manufacturers (that has led to more young smokers in Third World countries) become a public issue in the United States? Purposive attempts at agenda-setting by media personalities and organizations are often unsuccessful. Members of the U.S. media audience frequently reject the media's agenda of important issues. People "co-construct" what they see, read, and hear from the media with information drawn from their own lives (Neuman, Just, & Crigler, 1992) to create a meaning for some issue.

The Media Agenda, Public Agenda, and Policy Agenda

The agenda-setting process is composed of the media agenda, the public agenda, and the policy agenda, and the interrelationships among these three elements (Figure 1.1). A research tradition exists for each of these three types of agendas. The first research tradition is called *media agenda-setting* because its main dependent variable is the importance of an issue on the mass media agenda. The second research tradition is called *public agenda-setting* because its main dependent variable is the importance of a set of issues on the public agenda. The third research tradition is called *policy agenda-setting* because the distinctive aspect of this scholarly tradition is its concern with policy actions regarding an issue, in part as a response to the media agenda and the public agenda.

So, the agenda-setting process is an ongoing competition among the proponents of a set of issues to gain the attention of media professionals, the public, and policy elites. But agenda-setting was not originally conceptualized in this way.

The Chapel Hill Study[1]

The term *agenda-setting* first appeared in an influential article by Maxwell E. McCombs and Donald L. Shaw in 1972. These scholars at the University of North Carolina studied the role of the mass media in the 1968 presidential campaign in the university town of Chapel Hill, North Carolina. For their study, they selected 100 undecided voters because these voters were "presumably those most open or susceptible to campaign information." These respondents were personally interviewed in a 3-week period during September and October 1968, just prior to the election. The voters' public agenda of campaign issues was measured by aggregating their responses to a survey question: "What are you *most* concerned about these days? That is, regardless of what politicians say, what are the two or three *main* things that you think the government *should* concentrate on doing something about?" (McCombs & Shaw, 1972). Five main campaign issues (foreign policy, law and order, fiscal policy, public welfare, and civil rights) were mentioned most frequently by the 100 undecided voters, thus measuring the public agenda.

The media agenda was measured by counting the number of news articles, editorials, and broadcast stories in the nine mass media that served Chapel Hill. McCombs and Shaw found an almost perfect correlation between the rank order of (a) the five issues on the media agenda (measured by their content analysis of the media coverage of the election campaign) and (b) the same five issues on the public agenda (measured by their survey of the 100 undecided voters). For instance, foreign policy was ranked as the most important issue by the public, and this issue was given the most attention by the media in the period leading up to the election.

McCombs and Shaw concluded from their analysis that the mass media "set" the agenda for the public.[2] Presumably, the public agenda was important in the presidential election because it determined who one voted for, although McCombs and Shaw did not investigate any behavioral consequence of the public agenda.

What was the special contribution of the Chapel Hill study of agenda-setting? The methodologies for measuring the two conceptual variables were not new: Both (a) content analysis of mass media messages and (b) surveys of public opinion about an issue were by then common in mass communication research. McCombs and Shaw's linking of the two methodologies to test public agenda-setting was not a new contribution either. Twenty years earlier, F. James Davis (1952) had combined content analysis, survey research, and "real-world" indicators in testing the public agenda-setting hypothesis (although Davis had not called the process "agenda-setting"). A *real-world indicator* is a variable that measures more or less objectively the degree of severity or risk of a social problem. McCombs and Shaw's contribution was in clearly laying out the agenda-setting hypothesis, in calling the media-public agenda relationship "agenda-setting," in suggesting a paradigm for further research, and in training many excellent students who went on to carry out agenda-setting research of their own.

Salience as the Key in Agenda-Setting

Abortion is a highly charged, very emotional public issue in the United States. Should abortion be a legal option for pregnant women? Or should abortion be illegal? Many scholars study public attitudes about abortion by surveying a sample of people. Other scholars study portrayals of abortion on television news to determine whether media coverage favors one viewpoint over another. But an agenda-setting scholar studying the abortion issue in the U.S. media would ask, "*How important* is the abortion issue on television news?" "That is, how does the abortion issue compare with other issues in the amount of news coverage that it receives?" "Why is the abortion issue in the news?" "Why now?" A scholar might also ask individuals in a public opinion survey: "What is the most important problem facing the United States today? How about abortion?"

Salience is the degree to which an issue on the agenda is perceived as relatively important. The heart of the agenda-setting process is when the salience of an issue changes on the media agenda, the public agenda, or the policy agenda. The task of the scholar of agenda-setting is to measure how the salience of an issue changes, and why this change occurs.

Rather than focusing on positive or negative attitudes toward an issue, as most public opinion research does, agenda-setting scholars focus on the salience of an issue. This salience on the media agenda tells viewers, readers, and listeners "what issues to think about." Research on the agenda-setting process suggests that the relative salience of an issue on the media agenda determines how the public agenda is formed, which in turn influences which issues policymakers consider. Control of the choices available for action is a manifestation of power. Policymakers only act on those issues that reach the top of the policy agenda.

History of Agenda-Setting Research

Thomas Kuhn's (1962/1970) book *The Structure of Scientific Revolutions* provides one means for understanding the background of agenda-setting research. Our focus is on how the paradigm for agenda-setting research was formed and the time sequence in which the main components of this paradigm were introduced as conceptual innovations (Table 1.1).

Kuhn argues that the model of the development of a scientific specialty begins when scientists in a field are attracted to a new paradigm as a focus for their research. A *paradigm* is a scientific conceptualization that provides model problems and solutions to a community of scholars (Kuhn, 1962/1970, p. viii; Rogers, 1983, p. 43). Kuhn says that a scientific specialty does not advance in a series of small incremental steps as hypotheses are proposed, tested, and then revised, thus furthering knowledge. Instead, science moves forward in major jumps and starts. Pronounced discontinuities occur as a revolutionary paradigm is proposed; it offers an entirely new way of looking at some scientific problem.

Table 1.1 Development of the Paradigm for Research on the
Agenda-Setting Process

Theoretical and Methodological Innovations in Studying the Agenda-Setting Process	*Publication First Reporting the Scholarly Innovation*
1. Postulating a relationship between the mass media agenda and the public agenda	Walter Lippmann (1922)
2. Identifying the status-conferral function of the media, in which salience is given to issues	Paul F. Lazarsfeld and Robert K. Merton (1948/1964)
3. Stating the metaphor of agenda-setting	Bernard C. Cohen (1963)
4. Giving a name to the agenda-setting process	Maxwell McCombs and Donald Shaw (1972)
5. Investigating the public agenda-setting process for a hierarchy of issues	Maxwell McCombs and Donald Shaw (1972)
6. Explicating a model of the policy agenda-setting process	Roger W. Cobb and Charles D. Elder (1972/1983)
7. Initiating the over-time study of public-agenda-setting at a macro level of analysis, and investigating the relationship of real-world indicators to the media agenda	G. Ray Funkhouser (1973a)
8. Experimentally investigating public agenda-setting at a micro level of analysis	Shanto Iyengar and Donald R. Kinder (1987)

Famous examples are Copernicus's solar-centered universe, Einstein's relativity theory, Darwinian evolution, and Freud's psychoanalytic theory (most scientific paradigms are much less noteworthy than these examples).

Each new paradigm initially attracts a furious amount of intellectual activity as scientists seek to test the new conceptualization, either to advance the new theory or to disprove it. Gradually, over a period of time, an intellectual consensus about the new paradigm develops among scientists in a field through a verification process. Then, scientific interest declines as fewer findings of an exciting nature are reported. Kuhn (1962/1970) calls this stage "normal science." Research becomes a kind of mopping-up operation. Eventually, a yet newer paradigm may be proposed, setting off another scientific revolution, when anomalies in the existing paradigm are recognized by the "invisible college"[3] of

Table 1.2 The Rise and Fall of the Paradigm for Agenda-Setting Research

Stages in Kuhn's (1962/1970) Development of a Scientific Paradigm	Main Events in the Development of the Paradigm for Agenda-Setting Research
1. Preparadigmatic work appears.	Robert E. Park's (1922) *The Immigrant Press and Its Control,* Walter Lippmann's (1922) *Public Opinion,* and Bernard Cohen's (1963) *The Press and Foreign Policy*
2. The paradigm for agenda-setting research appears.	Maxwell McCombs and Donald Shaw (1972) create the paradigm in their Chapel Hill study, which McCombs then follows up with further research over future years.
3. Normal science: An invisible college forms around the paradigm.	Some 357 publications about agenda-setting appear from 1972 through 1994, in which the paradigm is supported and, in recent years, expanded in scope.
4. A decline in scholarly interest begins as the major research problems are solved, anomalies appear, and scientific controversy occurs.	This stage has not yet occurred for agenda-setting research.
5. Exhaustion, as scientific interest in the paradigm shifts to the newer paradigm that replaces it.	This stage has not yet occurred.

scholars investigating the scientific problem of study. Table 1.2 lists the paradigmatic history of agenda-setting research.

Robert E. Park, a sociologist at the University of Chicago from 1915 to 1935, and perhaps the first scholar of mass communication, conceived of media gatekeeping and implied what is today called the agenda-setting process:

> Out of all the events that happened and are recorded every day by correspondents, reporters, and the news agencies, the editor chooses certain items for publication which he regards as more important or more interesting than others. The remainder he condemns to oblivion and the waste basket. There is an enormous amount of news "killed" every day. (Park, 1922, p. 328)

Park was distinguishing between problems that become public issues and those that don't.

Walter Lippmann was a scholar of propaganda and public opinion who pioneered early thinking about agenda-setting. Among academics, this influential newspaper columnist and longtime presidential adviser is best known for his 1922 book *Public Opinion*, in which Lippmann wrote of "The World Outside and the Pictures in Our Heads." He argued that the mass media are the principal connection between (a) events that occur in the world and (b) the images of these events in our minds.

Lippmann did not earn a graduate degree at a university (although he did study at Harvard), he never taught a university class, and he never adopted the research methods or the theoretical perspectives of social science. Yet he was the single most influential writer about the role of the mass media in shaping public opinion, eventually setting off the research tradition on agenda-setting. Lippmann did not use the term agenda-setting, however (see Table 1.1); nor did he think that research was needed on this process.

Harold D. Lasswell, a political scientist at the University of Chicago, was one of the forefathers of communication study in the United States (Rogers, 1994). In a seminal 1948 chapter, Lasswell posed a five-part question that became a model for communication inquiry: *Who* says *what* to *whom* via *which channels* and with *what effect?* According to Lasswell, two of the most important functions that the mass media have in society are "surveillance" and "correlation." The surveillance function occurs when media newspeople scan their constantly changing information environment (alerted by police reports, announcements of local events, press releases, and such other sources as the Associated Press wire service) and decide which events should receive news attention. This weeding of potential stories via surveillance is now known as editorial gatekeeping (Shoemaker, 1991).

Lasswell's (1948) notion of the "correlation of the parts of society in responding to the environment" (p. 38) describes communication performing the vital function of enabling a living organism like a society to synchronize the importance accorded to an issue by its constituent parts (such as the mass media, attentive public groups, and elected officials). Lasswell (1948) wrote that mass media, public groups, and policymakers each have discrete "attention frames" or periods of time during which they pay attention to certain issues. Lasswell believed that the media play the critical role in directing our attention to issues. The result, he suggested, was a correlation of attention on certain issues at the same time by the media, the public, and policymakers. This idea was seized upon by McCombs and Shaw (1972) as the "agenda-setting function of the mass media."

Forty years after publication of Lippmann's *Public Opinion* and 15 years after Lasswell's seminal chapter, a political scientist, Bernard Cohen, inspired by the work of Schattschneider (1960), further advanced the conceptualization of agenda-setting. Cohen (1963) observed, as we noted at the top of this chapter, that the press

> may not be successful much of the time in telling people *what to think,* but it is stunningly successful in telling its readers *what to think about.* . . . The world will look different to different people, depending . . . on the map that is drawn for them by writers, editors, and publishers of the [news]paper they read. (p. 13, italics added)

Cohen thus expressed the metaphor that led to agenda-setting research (see Table 1.1).

Agenda-setting was, however, still simply a theoretical idea, yet unnamed. The 1972 study by McCombs and Shaw set off a research paradigm that was adopted mainly by mass communication scholars, and to a lesser extent by political scientists, sociologists, and other scholars. The paradigm offered a new way to think about the power of the mass media. Prior to 1972, the dominant scholarly approach in mass communication research was to look for the direct effects of media messages in changing the attitudes of individuals in the audience. However, few such directional media effects were found. Many early mass communication scholars (a number of whom had been newspaper journalists before they earned PhDs) believed that the mass media affected the public in important ways, but the empirical research findings of that time only indicated minimal media effects and did not support their personal convictions. This anomaly led to dismay with the paradigm of directional media effects and, as Kuhn (1962/1970) would predict (see Table 1.2), led to a search for a new paradigm.

The McCombs and Shaw article, with a spectacularly high rank-order correlation of +.98 between the salience of the five issues on the media agenda and their corresponding salience on the public agenda, provided empirical evidence that matched the scholars' beliefs about the power of the mass media. The media effects were cognitive rather than persuasive (which seemed reasonable to communication scholars with media experience, as newspapers should inform, giving both sides of an issue, rather than seek to persuade individuals in the audience of one position).

The McCombs and Shaw (1972) article is by far the most widely cited publication by agenda-setting scholars. Agenda-setting is one of the most popular topics in mass communication research, with about a dozen publications appearing each year for the past several decades. The paradigmatic study by McCombs and Shaw provided one means of empirically testing the media agenda-public agenda relationship, and thus of exploring an alternative paradigm to that of directional media effects. Their seminal article led not only to a proliferation of agenda-setting studies but to a wide variety of conceptual and methodological approaches. For the first 15 years or so after 1972, the invisible college of agenda-setting scholars were in Kuhn's "normal science" phase, in which most empirical studies build incrementally on previous work. In the 1970s, however, agenda-setting scholars began to break out of their rather stereotyped mold of conducting one-point-in-time content analyses of the media agenda and audience surveys of the public agenda (Shaw & McCombs, 1977; Weaver, Graber, McCombs, & Eyal, 1981). Later, some scholars traced a single issue (drug abuse or the environment) over time as a time-ordered process. Other scholars (Iyengar & Kinder, 1987) conducted laboratory experiments of the public agenda-setting process at the micro level of the individual (see Table 1.1). Respondents viewed doctored videos of evening television news broadcasts in which extra material was spliced in about a particular issue. As a result, the respondents subsequently ranked that issue higher on their agenda.

The Search for Media Effects

What attracts scholars to investigate agenda-setting? One main reason for the interest of mass communication researchers is that the agenda-setting paradigm appeared to offer an alternative to the scholarly search for directional media effects on individual attitudes and overt behavior change. Earlier mass communication research had found only limited media effects, which seemed counterintuitive to many mass communication researchers, especially to those who had previously worked in the mass media (Maxwell McCombs and Donald Shaw had both been newspaper reporters). Further, the early mass communication PhD graduates felt that the purpose of the media was mainly to inform rather than to persuade. So they looked for cognitive effects, like the agenda-setting process, in which people are primed concerning what issues to think about. Many of the agenda-setting publications by mass communication researchers stated their main justification as an attempt to overcome the limited-effects findings of past mass communication research. For example, Maxwell McCombs (1981a) stated in an overview:

Its [agenda-setting's] initial empirical exploration was fortuitously timed. It came at that time in the history of mass communication research when disenchantment both with attitudes and opinions as dependent variables, and with the limited-effects model as an adequate intellectual summary, was leading scholars to look elsewhere. (p. 121)

Many mass communication scholars were initially attracted to agenda-setting research as an alternative to looking for individual-level directional media effects, which had often been found to be minimal. Essentially, public agenda-setting research investigates an *indirect* effect ("what to think about") rather than a direct media effect ("what to think"). So the agenda-setting paradigm came along just when mass communication scholars were dismayed with their previous model of direct media effects, exactly as Thomas Kuhn (1962/1970) predicted should happen in a scientific revolution. The new paradigm sent mass communication researchers in the direction of studying how media news coverage affected an issue's salience, rather than directional media effects.

Recently, the contribution of agenda-setting research to understanding mass media effects was assessed:

Despite important shortcomings, the agenda-setting approach has contributed to a more advanced understanding of the media's role in society. . . . It has helped to change the emphasis of mass communication research away from the study of short-term attitudinal effects to a more longitudinal analysis of social impact. This is no small contribution. (Carragee, Rosenblatt, & Michaud, 1987, p. 42)

The agenda-setting effect is not the result of receiving one or a few messages but is due to the aggregate impact of a very large number of messages, each of which has a different content but all of which deal with the same general issue. For example, for 4 years after the first AIDS cases were reported in the United States (in 1981), the mass media carried very few news stories about the epidemic. The issue of AIDS was not yet on the media agenda, nor was the U.S. public very fully aware of the AIDS issue, so national poll results indicated. Then, in mid-1985, two news events (movie actor Rock Hudson's death from AIDS, and the refusal by the schools of Kokomo, Indiana, to allow a young boy with AIDS, Ryan White, to attend classes) suddenly led to a massive increase in media coverage of the AIDS issue. For example, six major media in the United States dramatically increased their coverage of AIDS from an average of 4 news stories per month to 15 news stories. The issue of AIDS climbed near the top of the national media agenda in early fall 1985. Almost immediately, public awareness of the epidemic increased until, in a few months, 95% of U.S. adults knew about AIDS and understood its means of transmission (Rogers et al., 1991).

In addition to the directional media effects tradition out of which it grew as an alternative, public agenda-setting research is related to the following research fronts:

1. Bandwagon effects (O'Gorman, 1975), through which knowledge of the public's opinion about some issue influences other individuals toward that opinion
2. The spiral of silence (Noelle-Neumann, 1984), through which the perception of majority opinion about an issue mutes the expression of alternative opinions
3. Social movements (Blumer, 1971; Gamson, 1992), through which people act collectively to see that solutions to social problems emerge and eventually are implemented
4. Propaganda analysis (e.g., Lasswell, 1927), through which persuasive messages shape public opinion
5. The diffusion of news events (DeFleur, 1987; Deutschmann & Danielson, 1960), the process through which an important news event such as the 1986 *Challenger* disaster or Magic Johnson's announcement that he had contracted HIV (the human immunodeficiency virus) is communicated to the public—usually such spectacular news events spread very rapidly to the public
6. Entertainment-education and Hollywood lobbying strategies (Montgomery, 1989, 1993; Shefner & Rogers, 1992), through which an educational issue such as drunk driving or the environment is purposively placed in entertainment messages within prime-time television shows or popular music

7. Media advocacy (Wallack, 1990), through which media coverage of a prosocial issue, such as the health threat of cigarette smoking, is purposively promoted
8. Media gatekeeping (Shoemaker, 1991), the process through which an individual controls the flow of messages through a communication channel (examples of media gatekeepers are a newspaper editor and a television news director)
9. Media-system dependency (Ball-Rokeach, 1985), in which mass media organizations are influenced by the environment of other organizations and institutions, thus affecting the messages that are communicated through the media

Intellectual boundaries are necessary for researchers to make sense of a topic of study and for a cumulative advance in understanding a research problem. Intellectual boundaries also inhibit learning between scholars working in different paradigms. The intellectual boundaries around the agenda-setting tradition should be broken down for a more comprehensive understanding of how social change occurs. Conflict, controversy, and negotiation (concepts that political scientists and international relations scholars use in understanding policy agenda-setting) could advance our grasp of the role of proponents on media, public, and policy agendas. Media agenda research demonstrates the interrelationships of a particular media organization with events in the larger social system of which it is a part. To influence the issues that get on a media organization's news agenda is to exercise *power*, the use of social influence. Understanding how democracy works can be better achieved by studying the power of issues rather than the issue of power. Thus, agenda-setting investigations have mainly been conducted by scholars of mass communication and of political science.

Three Research Traditions

Scholarly work on the agenda-setting process has evolved over the past 20 years as two distinct research fronts. One dealt mainly with *public* agenda-setting. The 1972 study by Maxwell McCombs and Donald Shaw set off this research tradition, which has been mainly conducted by mass communication scholars. More than 100 publications report empirical investigations of the relationship between the media agenda and its corresponding public agenda.

Generally unrelated to this stream of mass communication research on public agenda-setting is a research tradition on *policy* agenda-setting, mainly carried forward by political scientists and sociologists. Here the key question for political scientists such as John Kingdon (1984) is, "How does an issue get on the policy agenda?" and for sociologists such as Herbert Blumer (1971), "How does collective behavior coalesce around social problems?" Occasionally, they explicitly focus on the mass media by asking, "How may the mass media directly influence the policy agenda?" (Linsky, 1986). Because they recognize the role of networks of people who are linked together through concern about common issues, sociologists and political scientists have increasingly focused on the mobilization of resources by groups of people to affect policy change (Gamson, 1975; Lipsky, 1968; McCarthy & Zald, 1977).

How the *media* agenda is set has only been investigated in fairly recent years. Our review shows fewer than 20 such publications. "Agenda-setting research has consistently accepted the media agenda as a given without considering the process by which the agenda is constructed" (Carragee et al., 1987, p. 43). A variety of factors, including personality characteristics, news values, organizational norms and politics, and external sources affect the decision on "what's news" (Gans, 1979). Recent investigations show that (a) the *New York Times*, (b) the White House, (c) scientific journals, and (d) public opinion polling results play a particularly important role in putting an issue on the U.S. media agenda. These influential agenda-setters function to keep issues off the national agenda by ignoring them.

Measuring Agendas

Public, media, and policy agendas, and real-world indicators, are typically measured as follows:

1. The public agenda is usually measured by public opinion surveys in which a sample of individuals is asked a question originally designed by George Gallup: "What is the most important problem facing this country today?" The aggregated responses to such an MIP (most important problem) question indicate the relative position of an issue on the public agenda. For example, in 1989, 54% of a national sample of Americans said that drugs were the most important issue facing Amer-

ica; 2 years later, this number dropped to only 4%, as the "War on Drugs" was pushed down the agenda by other issues.

2. The media agenda is usually indexed by a content analysis of the news media to determine the number of news stories about an issue or issues of study (e.g., the War on Drugs). The *number* of news stories measures the relative salience of an issue of study on the media agenda. Audience individuals presumably judge the relative importance of an issue on the basis of the number of media messages about the issue to which they are exposed. Historically, the public agenda was measured first (the MIP question was first asked by George Gallup in 1935). The content analysis measure of the media agenda was derived by McCombs and Shaw (1972) and Funkhouser (1973a) as a parallel to the MIP measure of the public agenda, focusing similarly on issues.

3. The policy agenda for an issue or issues is measured by such policy actions as the introduction of laws about an issue, by budget appropriations, and by the amount of time given to debate of an issue in the U.S. Congress. Measures of the policy agenda vary from study to study much more than do measures of the media agenda or of the public agenda, which are fairly standard.

4. Real-world indicators are often conceptualized by agenda-setting scholars as a single-variable indicator, such as the number of drug-related deaths per year or the unemployment rate. Such real-world indicators are commonly accepted indexes of the severity of a social problem. Certain scholars constructed a composite real-world indicator made up of several component measures of an issue's severity. An example is Ader's (1993) real-world indicator for the environmental issue in the United States, which included variables for air pollution, oil spills, and solid waste (this study is reviewed in Chapter 2).

Certain agenda-setting studies seek to understand the temporal dynamics of the agenda-setting process by analyzing the relationships between the media agenda, the public agenda, the policy agenda, and real-world indicators over time rather than cross-sectionally (at one point in time). In such longitudinal studies, a qualitative over-time method such as participant observation or a quantitative over-time method such as time-series analysis may be used. Several different data-gathering methods may be used in conjunction to ensure that measures are (a) valid (i.e., the scholar is really measuring what he or she intends to measure) and (b) reliable (the same conclusions would be

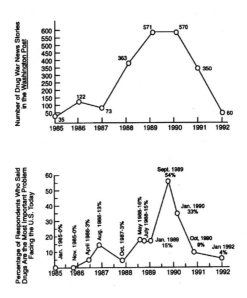

Figure 1.2. The Drug Issue on the U.S. Media Agenda (above) and on the Public Agenda (below)
SOURCE: Based on various sources.

reached with other methods or by other scholars). Such multiple measurement of concepts is called *triangulation*, a topic to which we shall return as multimethod research (see Chapter 6).

The Rise and Fall of the War on Drugs[4]

The issue of drug abuse rose gradually on the media agenda and the public agenda in the United States during the mid-1980s, with the drug-related death of basketball star Len Bias in 1986 and First Lady Nancy Reagan's "Just Say No" campaign propelling the drug issue up the national agenda (Danielian & Reese, 1989). Education about drug abuse prevention became a $2 billion a year "industry," with much of the funding coming from the federal government.

The "real-world indicator" of the number of drug-related deaths per year, however, actually *decreased* during the 1980s (Kerr, 1986)! Nevertheless, the drug issue peaked on the public agenda in September 1989, when the *New York Times*-CBS News Poll found that 54% of the U.S. public said that drug abuse was the most important problem facing the nation (Figure 1.2). By January 1992, 28 months later, only 4% of the U.S. public felt that drugs were the number one problem facing the nation. What explains this rapid rise and fall of the drug issue on the public agenda?

The media were reacting in part to a particular type of "real-world indicator": The use of cocaine in dangerous forms such as crack (Shoemaker, 1989, p. 4). Crack is smoked instead of snorted, creating a more immediate and more intense effect on the individual user. Crack cocaine is more addictive. Although crack had been used by some individuals in the United States for several years prior to 1986, it became more widely used in 1986.

Adam Weisman (1986), a Washington, D.C. journalist, in a *New Republic* article titled, "I Was a Drug-Hype Junkie," wrote: "For a reporter at a national news organization in 1986, the drug crisis in America is more than a story, it's an addiction—and a dangerous one" (p. 14). Why and how did the drug problem suddenly command so much media attention in 1986? Both the *New York Times* and the White House helped set the media agenda for the drug issue. The *New York Times* assigned a reporter to cover illegal drugs full-time in November 1985, shortly after the Reverend Jesse Jackson visited Abe Rosenthal, then the newspaper's executive director, to stress the drug problem. The *Times* carried its first front-page story about crack cocaine on November 29, 1985 (Kerr, 1986). When the *Times* considers an issue newsworthy, other U.S. media are influenced to follow suit.

The death of All-American basketball star Len Bias on June 19, 1986, had a strong impact on the national agenda because he played for the University of Maryland: "The death of the young basketball player, in particular, had a startling impact on the nation's capital, where Maryland is virtually a home team" (Kerr, 1986, p. 1). On the day of his death, Bias had signed a professional contract with the Boston Celtics for $6 million. The death of such a promising young basketball player humanized the drug issue.

The media responded to the death of Len Bias and to White House influences with a "crack attack": Much of the media coverage dealt with the new, more dangerous way of ingesting cocaine.

Media coverage of crack cocaine increased sharply in 1986. *Time* magazine devoted five 1986 cover stories to the crack crisis. CBS News with Dan Rather broadcast a dramatic two-hour documentary, "48 Hours on Crack Street." The media used words like *crisis, plague,* and *epidemic* to describe the drug problem in America. The Associated Press annual survey of editors rated the drug problem as the ninth most important news story of 1986.

Did the extensive and sensationalistic media coverage of the drug problem influence public opinion? Shoemaker, Wanta, and Leggett (1989) found that the percentage of the American public saying that drugs was "the most important problem facing America today" in 43 Gallup Polls from 1972 to 1986 was positively correlated with the amount of media coverage given to the drug issue a few months prior to each poll. An April 1986 national poll sponsored by the *New York Times* and CBS News found that 3% of American adults considered drugs to be the nation's most important problem. Five months later, in August 1986, following the intense media coverage of the death of Len Bias and the public campaigns organized by the National Institute on Drug Abuse (including its "Just Say No" campaign led by First Lady Nancy Reagan), 13% of American adults said that drugs were the nation's most important problem (Kerr, 1986). Three years later, in September 1989, 54% of the public rated drugs as the number one problem facing America (see Figure 1.2).

The intense media coverage of drugs influenced both public opinion and policy decisions. From 1981 to 1987, federal funding for antidrug law enforcement tripled, from $1 billion to $3 billion. An additional $5 billion was spent in 1987 by state and local law enforcement agencies, about one-fifth of their total budget. Federal funding for drug abuse prevention programs increased through the National Institute for Drug Abuse (NIDA), the Office of Substance Abuse Prevention (OSAP), the U.S. Department of Education, and the U.S. Department of Justice (to local police departments for D.A.R.E. training—5 million schoolchildren were trained in these drug abuse prevention programs by 1990).

So the agenda-setting process for the drug issue in the mid- to late 1980s can be characterized as one in which the issue climbed to a high priority on the media agenda, then shot up the public agenda, and finally climbed the policy agenda, without any increase in the real-world indicator of the overall drug problem in the United States. Although an increase occurred in the abuse of one cocaine derivative, crack, other, equally harmful types of drug abuse declined.

Why did the drug issue drop down the public agenda after 1989? Media overexposure may be one reason; the heavy media coverage of the drug issue may have led the public to think that the problem was being handled by the government. Also, drugs were pushed down the national agenda by other issues, especially America's economic difficulties in the 1980s and the 1991 Gulf War.

The rise and fall of the drug issue on the national agenda in the late 1980s suggests that the agenda-setting process for this issue was a social construction, bearing little relationship to the objective indicator of deaths due to drugs in the United States. This social construction of the drug issue was mainly driven by the mass media.

Summary

The *agenda-setting process* is an ongoing competition among issue proponents to gain the attention of media professionals, the public, and policy elites. An *issue* is a social problem, often conflictual, that has received media coverage. Agenda-setting can be a zero-sum game in that space on the agenda is a scarce resource, and so a new issue must push another issue down the agenda to come to attention. We see agenda-setting as a political process in which the mass media play a crucial role in enabling social problems to become acknowledged as public issues.

Our model of the agenda-setting process consists of three main components: (a) the media agenda, which influences (b) the public agenda, which in turn may influence (c) the policy agenda. *Salience* is the degree to which an issue on the agenda is perceived as relatively important. The key question for agenda-setting scholars is why the salience of an issue on the media agenda, public agenda, and policy agenda increases or decreases. The public agenda is often measured by public opinion surveys in which individuals are asked what the most important question facing the nation is, and less often by studying the over-time activities of social movements, grassroots organizing, and consumer groups. The media agenda is usually measured by a content analysis of media news coverage of an issue or issues. The policy agenda is measured by such policy actions as the introduction of new laws about an issue, budget appropriations, and other legislative decisions.

A fourth variable has often been studied in agenda-setting investigations: a *real-world indicator*, defined as a variable that measures more or less objectively the degree of severity or risk of a social problem. Such objective indicators as the number of annual traffic deaths or the rate of inflation have generally been found to be relatively unimportant in putting an issue on the media agenda. Salience on the media agenda usually boosts an issue on the public agenda, as people take cues from the amount of media coverage to judge the salience of an issue (the public agenda).

Notes

1. This case illustration is based on Maxwell E. McCombs and Donald L. Shaw (1972).

2. However, two immediate retests of the media agenda-public agenda hypothesis using different research designs from McCombs and Shaw found only moderate support (McLeod, Becker, & Byrnes, 1974; Tipton, Haney, & Baseheart, 1975). Our meta-research of 92 empirical studies of the media agenda-public agenda relationship found support for the McCombs-Shaw hypothesis in 59 studies, about two thirds of the investigations.

3. An *invisible college* is the informal network of scholars who are often spatially dispersed but who investigate the same paradigm (Crane, 1972; Price, 1961).

4. This case illustration is adapted from a variety of sources but draws especially on the book edited by Pamela J. Shoemaker (1989).

2. *Media Agenda Studies*

> The mass media *confer* status on public issues, persons, organiza-
> tions and social movements.
>
> Paul F. Lazarsfeld and
> Robert K. Merton (1948/1964, p. 101)

As the above quotation from Lazarsfeld and Merton states, the media confer attention on both people and issues. Communication scholars since 1948 have given most attention to status conferred by the media to people. For example, introductory textbooks in mass communication frequently provide the example of how appearing on the cover of *Time* magazine confers star status on an individual. But the other status-conferral function of the media, calling attention to an *issue*, is much more important in understanding how American democracy works. This can happen in roundabout ways. For example, in November 1995, CBS lawyers prohibited Mike Wallace of *60 Minutes* from airing an interview with a tobacco industry whistle-blower. The corporation's action led to a flurry of news stories by other mass media organizations, all of which raised the problem (of risk-averse decision making in mass media organizations due to the influence of corporate lawyers) to "issue status."

The agenda-setting process begins with an issue climbing the media agenda. What puts an issue on the media agenda? In the first decade or so of agenda-setting research, this question was relatively unexplored by communication scientists. Scholars took the media agenda as a given as they investigated the media agenda-public agenda relationship. Then, at the 1980 International Communication Association meeting, Steve Chaffee pointed to the important question of how the media agenda was set. Shortly, communication research began on this topic, especially in the new single-issue studies of agenda-setting that emerged in the 1980s (see Chapter 4).

Understanding the wide array of influences on mass media decision makers as media agenda-setting is attractive to scholars because of the theoretical rationale that agenda-setting brings to other paradigms that have evolved for studying influence, such as the role of salience cues and responses to them by media gatekeepers, the sociology of work in news organizations, and how news and entertainment sources seek to appeal to the values and practices of mass media personnel to gain attention. The sources of news are (as we suggested in Chapter 1) issue proponents, for the purpose of pushing a cause, promoting a vision or value system, or publicizing an organization. Benefits of getting on mass media agendas also accrue to individuals through recognition and reward.

Research also has shown that the U.S. president and the *New York Times* are important in setting the media agenda for national issues, Congress is able to set the media agenda to a lesser degree (Goodman, 1994), and real-world indicators are often not important. Do these research findings mean that media advocacy is futile, or that media advocates can only push an issue up the media agenda by influencing the chief executive to give a speech about the issue or to get a news story about the issue on the front page of the *New York Times?* Not for the issue of drunk driving, as the following case illustration of the Harvard Alcohol Project shows.

Media Advocacy for Drunk Driving[1]

Jay A. Winsten is Professor of Public Health in the Center for Health Communication of the Harvard School of Public Health. In the mid-1980s, Winsten traveled to Stockholm to study Sweden's drunk driving policies. He became especially interested in the idea of the "designated driver": When several Swedes go out drinking together, they select one of their number to serve as their non-drinking chauffeur.

Soon thereafter, a popular Boston television news anchor was killed by a drunk driver, leaving a wife and young child as survivors. An outpouring of grief at the funeral, attended by many Boston-area newspersons, led Winsten to launch a media campaign in Boston for the designated driver concept. A couple of years later, in 1987, Winsten asked Frank Stanton, former president of CBS and an adviser to Harvard's Center for Health Communication, to telephone Grant Tinker, a former NBC network executive who headed a Hollywood television studio, about launching a national designated driver campaign. Tinker in turn called or wrote each of the television production studio heads in Los Angeles, urging them to meet with Winsten.

During 1988, Winsten made numerous trips to Los Angeles, where he met personally with scriptwriters and executive producers of prime-time television shows, urging them to incorporate the concept of the designated driver in an episode or at least to mention the idea. Winsten spent 25 workweeks in Hollywood, promoting the Harvard Alcohol Project. The first annual designated driver campaign began in November 1988, with the episodes broadcast over the Thanksgiving-Christmas-New Year's holidays, a period of particularly heavy drinking in America.

Winsten's style of media advocacy is based on the *entertainment-education strategy*, the placing of subtle educational messages in entertainment programs rather than lecturing or preaching about an educational point. The advantages of the designated driver idea were shown through the behavior of role models on prime-time television series. One advantage is that a large audience is exposed to the educational message, which is acted out by the characters in the entertainment program. For example, on April 12, 1989, ABC aired a shocking episode of its popular situation comedy *Growing Pains*. A teenage boy, after having several drinks, was seriously injured in a drunk driving auto crash. The youth promises, from his hospital bed, not to drink and drive again, thankful for a "second chance." In the episode's dramatic ending, the teenager dies (without a second chance). The age of the television character was important: Alcohol-related traffic deaths are the leading cause of fatalities for individuals ages 15 to 24.

Television scriptwriters inserted drunk driving prevention messages into such top-rated television programs as *Cheers, L.A. Law,* and *The Cosby Show*. Over the next 4 years, the Harvard Alcohol Project caused 140 prime-time television programs to include subplots, scenes, and dialogue about the designated driver. Thirty complete episodes focused on the designated driver. The three television networks also aired frequent public service announcements (PSAs) during prime-time hours, encouraging the use of the designated driver idea. The Harvard Alcohol Project annually received more than $100 million worth of network airtime, while costing only $300,000 (these funds were contributed by grants from private foundations).

Public opinion polls conducted since the first designated driver campaign show a wide acceptance of the concept. Roper polls found that 37% of Americans reported in 1991 that they had actually been a designated driver. Some 28% of alcohol drinkers have been driven home by a designated driver. In the first 4 years of the annual designated driver campaigns, alcohol-related traffic fatalities declined by approximately 20%, compared with a 0% decline in the three years immediately preceding the first designated driver campaign in 1988. Part of this decline probably was due to the Harvard Alcohol Project.

Why was the media advocacy by Jay Winsten successful in promoting the designated driver concept?

1. The annual designated driver campaigns built on important social changes already under way in the United States. The federal government and a powerful private organization, MADD (Mothers Against Drunk Driving), had already instigated a strong movement against drunk driving in the early 1980s (Reinarman, 1988). Social problems that are portrayed or framed in terms of issues about which people are already thinking are more likely to be noticed and perceived as relevant. This selective nature of human perception means that the timing of information campaigns by issue proponents is important.

2. The designated driver campaign was spearheaded by a prestigious institution, Harvard University. Winsten capitalized on the credibility of Harvard in various persuasive ways, rewarding Hollywood officials and scriptwriters with Harvard paperweights and other insignia when the designated driver concept appeared in their television shows.

3. The Harvard Alcohol Project was a top-down campaign with strong support from respected industry leaders. Frank Stanton and Grant Tinker were television heavyweights. Top-down, centralized campaigns are often ineffective when cooperation with individuals and grassroots organizations is necessary to carry out a campaign. Here, no bottom-up "buy-in" was necessary for the campaign to occur.

28

4. The Harvard Alcohol Project attacked drunk driving, but it did not oppose alcoholism or the sale of alcoholic beverages, whose advertising is a very important source of income for the television industry.

The Harvard Alcohol Project has implications for agenda-setting research. Entertainment media and advertising (such as the PSAs for the designated driver concept) can play a role in agenda-setting, along with the news media. Past communication research has looked only at the amount of *news* coverage given an issue. Further, Jay Winsten's designated driver campaign suggests that a media advocate working as an issue proponent can boost an issue up the media agenda, especially if the advocate has a marketable "product" (in this case, the designated driver concept), knows powerful people, and has several hundred thousand dollars to spend.

Real-World Indicators and the Media Agenda

As defined previously, a *real-world indicator* is a variable that measures more or less objectively the degree of severity or risk of a social problem. Examples of real-world indicators are the number of alcohol-related traffic fatalities as well as unemployment and inflation rates. Most issues have potential indicators of their objective severity or risk as a social problem. Often, the indicator is a single variable. For certain issues that have several dimensions, such as the environment, a multiple-variable measure must be developed.

Christine Ader (1993) constructed a real-world indicator for the general environmental degradation problem in the United States by combining (a) air pollution, measured as the amount of sulfur oxides, nitrogen oxides, carbon monoxide, and total suspended particulates, measured in million metric tons per year; (b) oil spills in million metric tons; and (c) solid waste, measured in million metric tons disposed of per year. Her total pollution index summed these three components, with the total expressed in million metric tons. This real-world indicator displays a rather consistent decrease from 1970 through 1990. It is, however, *negatively* related ($r = -.796$) with the media agenda (measured by the amount of media coverage of the environmental issue on a year-by-year basis for the 20 years of study). In other words, as the problem of pollution decreased, media coverage of the issue increased!

Other researchers also have found no relationship, or a negative correlation, between real-world indicators and the media agenda. Consider the "War on Drugs" in the late 1980s, which, as mentioned in Chapter 1, occurred despite a long-term downward trend in deaths due to drugs. A key event in the agenda-setting process for the drug issue occurred in 1985 when the Reverend Jesse Jackson, head of the Rainbow Coalition and an aspiring presidential candidate, talked with the chief editor of the *New York Times* about the seriousness of the drug issue for black inner-city youth (see Chapter 1). Shortly thereafter, the *New York Times* "discovered" the drug issue, and numerous news stories about drugs appeared in the *Times*. Meanwhile, the number of drug-related deaths in the United States was actually decreasing during the 1980s. But with the drug overdose death of All-American basketball player Len Bias, the drug issue was framed by the U.S. media not as a matter of death rates but as one of human tragedy. Trends in a statistical index do not necessarily make a very dramatic news story compared with pictures of a sobbing mother at her son's grave.

The drug issue in the 1980s was a stark example of how the agenda-setting process can operate independently of real-world indicators. The drug problem of America in the 1980s was a kind of natural experiment in the social construction of an issue. Drugs were a serious problem, and they continue to be, as measured by objective indicators. Were this not the case, drugs could not have climbed the national agenda in the 1980s. So, a real-world indicator is neither a necessary nor a sufficient cause for an issue to climb the agenda. Certainly, an increase in a rate measure like the number of drunk driving deaths in America or drug-related deaths per year is not enough alone to boost an issue up the agenda. Agenda-setting often comes from a human tragedy like the death of a celebrity or from a spectacular news event like the U.S. government closing down for a few days due to a budget crisis (as happened in 1996). And an issue's boost up the agenda is often due to the efforts of an issue proponent like Jay Winsten, whether we know of their work or not. Real-world indicators alone seldom put an issue on the media agenda.

AIDS and the Media Agenda in San Francisco[2]

During the first decade following the May 1981 outbreak of the epidemic, the San Francisco media carried more stories about acquired immunodeficiency syndrome (AIDS) than did the media serving any other U.S. metropolitan area. Why did the issue of AIDS rise to the top of the San Francisco media agenda? And does a local agenda-setting process differ from a national agenda-setting process?

Compared with other U.S. cities, San Francisco's population is liberal and progressive and displays a "live-and-let-live" philosophy with tolerance for diverse lifestyles. These qualities made San Francisco a magnet for gay men in the mid-1970s. In 1974, police harassment of gays was halted by the city government (Fitzgerald, 1986). This "coming of rights" was important for the already large gay and lesbian population of the City by the Bay. San Francisco became a place where gays could publicly declare their sexual orientation without fear of reprisal. Word spread in gay newspapers across the United States that San Francisco was *the* place in which to live. Between 1974 and 1982, approximately 5,000 gays per year moved to the city. New arrivals settled in "the Castro," a one- by one-half-mile district, making it the major center of gay life in America. The 1982 gay population of San Francisco was estimated at 100,000; 40% of all men in San Francisco were gay. This population was the most formidable voting bloc in San Francisco.

In early 1981, the San Francisco medical community became aware of a strange immunity problem of otherwise healthy gay men. Gay medical doctors responded quickly by joining with the San Francisco Department of Public Health to trace the first signs of the AIDS epidemic. A bitter controversy swirled around a Department of Public Health plan to close local bathhouses to limit the spread of AIDS. Many gays in San Francisco interpreted the health authorities' attempts to stop the spread of the human immunodeficiency virus as a violation of their individual civil rights. Angry protests against closing the baths were supported by local gay newspapers, in which the bathhouses were heavy advertisers. This controversy made AIDS the number one political issue in San Francisco in the early 1980s, several years before AIDS became an important issue on the national agenda.

Why did the issue of AIDS climb the San Francisco media agenda? The major influences were (a) the highest rate of HIV infection of any North American city; (b) a strong commitment to the issue by several local journalists; (c) the network of gays and medical professionals who organized for self-help, such as by forming nonprofit organizations for HIV/AIDS prevention; (d) the political importance and economic affluence of gays in the city; and (e) a mayor and a city council who provided major funding for AIDS prevention, research, testing, and treatment. The political controversy between conservative gays, who interpreted AIDS as a threat to their personal rights, and liberal gays, who interpreted AIDS as a public health crisis, added political conflict to a medical mystery—story angles that the city's journalists found irresistible.

As a result, San Francisco was the first city in the world where the problem of HIV transmission and AIDS got on the agenda and became a public issue. Here, the real-world indicator of AIDS cases and the media agenda rose together, connected by a set of inter-mediary factors (political, demographic, and media related) that were unique to San Francisco. The importance of citizen organiz-ing and grassroots advocacy—the attentive and active public working to boost an issue that they have mobilized around—was of key importance in this local case. When active people organize into advocacy "issue networks" (Heclo, 1978), especially at local levels, organized publics can have more impact than mass media on policy agendas (Schweitzer & Smith, 1991).

Influencing the Media Agenda

Researchers have investigated a variety of influences on the mass media, including the role of advertisers, public relations staff, technical sources of information such as scientists, and other media. As shown in Chapter 1's Figure 1.1, certain prestigious media and specific news events play particularly important roles in boosting an issue up the media agenda. Examples of this point are provided in our case illustrations.

The *New York Times* is generally regarded as the most respected U.S. news medium. When the *Times* indicates that an issue is newsworthy, other U.S. news organizations take note. When producers and editors at television stations, radio stations, newspapers, and, to a lesser degree, newsmagazines sit down to decide which stories will receive the most time, the best placement, and the biggest headlines that day, they often have checked first to see what decisions the editors at the *Times* have made about the same issues. The *New York Times* news service conveys the next day's front-page stories to thousands of other newspapers, broadcasting stations, and other media institutions late each day, thus influencing the next morning's headlines and news priorities. Evidence of the agenda-setting power of the *New York Times* has been provided by various investigations. The news of the toxicological disaster at Love Canal was covered regularly by the daily newspapers of Buffalo and Niagara Falls, New York, for more than a year, but outside of the immediate area, no one paid much attention to the dangerous health effects of the underground chemical wastes on the families living in the Love Canal area. Then this issue was reported in a news story appearing on the front page of the *New York Times*. Immediately, state and federal health and environmental agencies sprang into action, launching programs to assist Love Canal residents. The issue of Love Canal then received major attention by the U.S. media for several months (Ploughman, 1984).

Media coverage of radon, a radioactive gas that can reach dangerous levels in a home's basement, displayed a similar pattern to that for Love Canal. The radon problem, originally concentrated in New Jersey and Eastern Pennsylvania, regularly received front-page coverage by the *Philadelphia Inquirer* and other local media. But radon did not get on the national media agenda. Then, after a year or so, a news story about radon appeared in the *New York Times*. The radon issue suddenly gained national media attention and climbed the public agenda, and state and federal programs were launched (Mazur, 1987).

As described in Chapter 1, the War on Drugs began climbing the media agenda after the Reverend Jesse Jackson pointed out this social problem to a senior editor of the *New York Times*. Within a year of the *Times*'s discovery of the drug issue, a famous basketball star died from a drug overdose, and the War on Drugs was on its way to the top of the national agenda. In contrast, the newspaper did *not* give much media coverage to the issue of AIDS until several years after the first AIDS cases were diagnosed in 1981 (see Chapter 4). This lack of coverage by the *New York Times* kept the AIDS issue from climbing the media agenda in the United States (Roger et al., 1991).

Why is the *New York Times* so influential in the agenda-setting process in the United States? One reason is that newspeople operate in a special kind of environment, without much contact with their audience members. So they take their clues about an issue's priority from other media. "Journalists communicate with an audience they cannot see or hear. It is a one-way conversation. They operate in a professional world inhabited mainly by news sources, public-relations specialists, and other journalists" (Neuman et al., 1992, p. 3).

The *New York Times* is one gateway for an issue onto the national media agenda. For most issue proponents, it is a tough gateway to get through. The White House is another very selective gateway. The U.S. president can help put an issue on the national agenda by giving a major policy address about it. In the case of AIDS in the 1980s, President Reagan helped delay the rise of the epidemic on the media agenda simply by ignoring it. As shown later in this chapter, federal expenditures for AIDS-related research, prevention, and treatment posed a threat to President Reagan's attempts to cut the domestic budget. The White House ignored the epidemic for as long as it could, a delay that probably led to the loss of many human lives.

The way in which the media frame an issue also determines whether it climbs the media agenda or falls back down. For instance, AIDS was originally framed by the media as a gay issue, as many of the first individuals to contract AIDS were gays. Initially, AIDS was called "GRID," for "Gay-Related Immunodeficiency Syndrome." It was soon realized, however, that the virus could be transmitted by blood transfusions, by heterosexual contact, and by sharing drug needles as well as by homosexual contact. Then the media framed the AIDS problem as mainly affecting certain segments of the U.S. population, but not as a threat to everyone. Such framing of the issue affected the news value of the epidemic in the early 1980s.

Similarity of Media Coverage of an Issue

Given the daily cross-checking by editors at different media organizations, you would expect communication scholars to have found a high degree of similarity between how one mass medium covers an issue and the amount of coverage given to the same issue by other media, and they

34

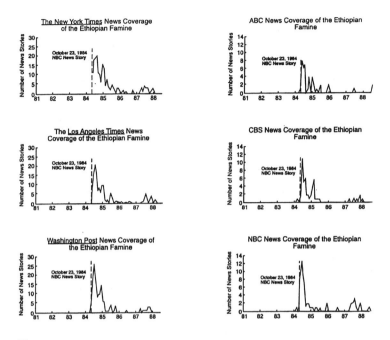

Figure 2.1. Three U.S. Newspapers Covered the Ethiopian Famine With a High Degree of Consistency in the Issue's Salience Over Time, as Did the Three U.S. Television Networks

SOURCE: Rogers and Chang (1991). From *Risky Business*, reproduced by permission of Greenwood Publishing Group, Inc., Westport, CT.

have. An illustration of this point is provided by the way in which three national newspapers and the three U.S. television networks covered the Ethiopian famine (described in Chapter 4). The six distributions of the number of news stories about this disaster over time are strikingly similar (Figure 2.1). The evening television programs carried about half as many news stories as did newspapers, but the over-time distribution of television coverage was almost identical to that of newspaper coverage. Figure 2.1 shows that the Ethiopian famine shot up the media agenda immediately after NBC broadcast a 3½-minute news film about the starving people in Ethiopia on October 23, 1984. This issue remained on the media agenda for the next year or two, although with a gradual falling off in news coverage, until the Ethiopian famine dropped off the media agenda entirely in 1989.

Note that the six national media were not necessarily saying exactly the same thing about the famine (although the media usually generally agree in how they frame a particular issue). But the media agreed on the news value of the Ethiopian drought, indicated by the relative number of news stories they devoted to this issue on a day-to-day basis.

This is intermedia agenda-setting at work. In addition to daily cross-checking of each other's prioritization of stories, there is a high degree of similarity in professional values among national newspeople. Almost all graduated from university schools of journalism and mass communication, where they took similar courses, read similar textbooks, and experienced similar internships in media institutions. Many of these national newspeople then worked together at one time or another during their careers. There is a high degree of job mobility in the news media. So, it is hardly surprising that national newspeople generally agree on the news value accorded a particular issue.

Measuring the Media Agenda

Content analysis is the quantification of meaning in documents. Meaning may be both manifest (that is, obvious) or latent (implied or inferred). A content analyst develops different measurement procedures depending on the type of meaning to be measured. For agenda-setting studies, media content is usually operationalized as *the number* of some countable unit, such as the number of story column inches in a set of newspapers, the number of front-page stories an issue receives, or the number of seconds about an issue during a year of TV newscasts. Often, the number of news stories about an issue of study is counted for a particular period of time, usually the several months prior to the measurement of the public agenda, by means of a poll or survey. The several months are needed because a lag factor usually occurs between media coverage and its impact on public opinion, as Eyal (1979), Eyal, Winter, and DeGeorge (1981), and Stone and McCombs (1981) found. In an over-time study of the agenda-setting process for a single issue, media coverage of the issue is usually tabulated for each month. In the case illustration of the agenda-setting process for the AIDS issue (in Chapter 4), Rogers et al. (1991) content-analyzed the number of news stories about AIDS in three national newspapers and three television networks during 91 months in the 1980s. Then, they compared this media agenda index with poll data on the public agenda, federal expenditures for AIDS programs, and other variables on a month-by-month basis.

Notice that in typical agenda-setting research, just the *number* of news reports about an issue are counted, not the exact *content* of these news stories. So, the media agenda is a rather gross indicator of the coverage accorded an issue. Repetition sets the public agenda through the continual hammering away of the media on the same issue. Of course, each news story about the issue of study is a variation on a theme, as each story describes some particular facet of the broad issue.

Studying the content within stories allows us to better understand the agenda-setting process. For instance, Rogers et al. (1991) counted the number of news reports about each of 13 themes of the issue of AIDS (such as scientific discoveries, mandatory testing for HIV/AIDS, famous people with AIDS, and children with AIDS). They found that themes rose and fell at different times. Together, this meant that it was these different story themes that enabled the overall issue of AIDS to remain high on the media agenda for 5 years in a row.

Typically, issues do not stay important on the media agenda for very long. Finding, counting, and coding thousands of stories, let alone analyzing the meaning of each story, is a very tedious task. Many scholars of agenda-setting cope with this information overload by using an index that is available for certain media of study. For example, the *Los Angeles Times Index* classifies all of the news articles and editorials that are published each year in the *Los Angeles Times,* providing the day of publication and the page number of that day's paper on which the news item appeared. Originally, this index was created to assist *Times* newspeople in locating past coverage of an issue. Say that a *Times* reporter is writing a news story about the death of tennis star Arthur Ashe due to AIDS. The reporter wants to read how the *Times* covered the earlier death of Rock Hudson. Thus, the reporter would consult the *Los Angeles Times Index* to identify such news coverage, and then read the news articles, which are stored on microfiche. This index, and the similar indexing service provided by other major newspapers, is a tremendous labor-saver for agenda-setting scholars.

An index is also available for ABC, NBC, and CBS evening television news programs, along with CNN newscasts. This index is produced by the Vanderbilt Television News Archive at Vanderbilt University in Nashville, and it identifies the topic of each television news story, the order in which it appeared in a particular program, and its length in minutes and seconds. This archive also keeps videotapes of all news-casts. They will sell you tapes of the newscasts for a certain issue as listed in their index. University Microfilms, in Minnesota, produces indexes for many U.S. newspapers.

The usefulness of media indexes as measures of the media agenda to scholars of the agenda-setting process depends upon how the medium's news stories were originally classified by the medium's indexers. Do the indexers who create the *Los Angeles Times Index* conceptualize issues in the same way that agenda-setting scholars do? Moreover, when we use indexes, our data can only be as accurate as the accuracy of the indexes themselves.

In Japan, Takeshita (1993) measured the media agenda for a small city by content-analyzing each line of the news articles appearing in the city's four main newspapers. These newspapers had quite different circulation rates, ranging from 44% of the households down to 2%. Accordingly, the media coverage of seven issues for each newspaper was weighted by the newspaper's circulation. Such weighting of the media agenda makes sense, but it is not clear whether the weighted media agenda was that much different from an unweighted media agenda. One reason not to weight elements in a media agenda is that it adds to the information overload faced by a scholar of the agenda-setting process.

In recent years, the tiring "eyeball" methods of content analysis of the media agenda are being replaced by use of computer software that can count stories, identify words in text when they appear together (this is called "co-word analysis"), and even assist the researcher in qualitative analysis of text. Instead of poring over thousands of pages of old newspapers, the contemporary scholar of the media agenda may instead choose to devise a set of computer commands in which the parameters of a computer search are carefully defined.

The Exxon *Valdez* and the Environment[3]

Twenty years after the environmental movement of the late 1960s, this issue again got on the national agenda in 1989. Compared with other national issues, the 1990s environmental issue was unique in the sense that it was multifaceted, including such subissues as ozone depletion, loss of rain forests, air and water pollution, endangered species, and recycling. Further, the ultimate source of information about the environment consists mainly of scientists, which means that scientifically based knowledge must be translated to the public. The environmental crisis, if it is to be solved, must be solved through the everyday actions of the mass public.

Prior to the 1989 Exxon *Valdez* oil spill, several real-world indicators suggested that a gradual worsening of the global environment was occurring. Scientists detected a growing hole in the ozone layer protecting the earth, and measured a gradual warming of the earth. Such real-world indicators of environmental problems were reported by the news media, scientific conferences were held, and heads of state discussed national environmental problems. But these real-world indicators of environmental degradation were gradual and long term. They did not put the environment on the national agenda.

On March 24, 1989, the Exxon *Valdez* tanker ran aground in Alaska's Prince William Sound, spilling 11 million gallons of crude oil into an ecologically fragile coastline area. The 987-foot tanker was headed for Long Beach, California, with a cargo of Alaska North Slope crude oil. The largest oil spill in U.S. waters rapidly spread across an area larger than the state of Rhode Island. The Exxon *Valdez* was under the command of Captain Joseph Hazelwood, who, at the time his ship ran aground, was resting below deck, allegedly under the influence of alcohol.

The magnitude of the Exxon *Valdez* disaster was headline news for many weeks following the spill. Television and print media carried photographs of the ocean blackened with oil, dead sea birds, and whimpering sea otters fighting for their lives. The disaster was a highly visual news story, perfect for television coverage. Wildlife damage, estimated 2 years after the spill, consisted of 580,000 dead birds (including 144 bald eagles), 22 whales, 5,500 sea otters, and 1,200 miles of Alaska coastline coated with crude oil. The oil spill received massive media coverage.

Environmental organizations, community groups, and politicians appealed to the public via the media to boycott all Exxon products. Exxon credit card holders were urged to cut their credit cards in half and send them to the corporation. More than 18,000 credit cards were returned to Exxon headquarters. In addition to the major *news* attention given to the Exxon *Valdez* incident and to the environmental crisis, *entertainment* media also gave increased attention to the environmental issue, in part as a result of the activities of two Hollywood lobbying organizations. EMA (Environmental Media Association) seeks to get the environmental crisis mentioned in U.S. television series and films. Another environmental lobbying organization, ECO (Earth Communications Office), was also founded in 1989. ECO organized a study trip to the Amazon rain forest led by actors John Ritter and Tom Cruise. Like EMA, ECO conducts fund-raising and other events to influence the Hollywood creative community to portray environmentally aware behavior and to give continued visibility to the environmental issue.

The massive media attention given to the Exxon *Valdez* incident and to other aspects of the environmental crisis convinced the U.S. public that the environment was an important issue facing the nation. The impacts of this disaster over the following months adversely affected the Exxon Corporation, boosted the environmental issue on the media agenda and the public agenda in the United States, and helped dramatize the environmental movement, leading to widespread behavioral changes on the part of the U.S. public. The March 1989 oil spill was the trigger event[4] that put the environmental issue on the media agenda, the public agenda, and the policy agenda. This spectacular event gave sudden symbolic significance to the scientifically documented social problem that had been gradually worsening for many years.

Summary

We ask a central question in this chapter: What puts an issue on the media agenda? We conclude that real-world indicators are sometimes a necessary but certainly not a sufficient explanation of media agenda-setting. Two institutions have been found to play a particularly crucial role in media agenda-setting for many national issues in the United States: the *New York Times* and the White House. Thereafter, the amount of news coverage given to an issue over a period of time by various mass media is very similar. The media agenda-setting process for an issue

40

usually is sparked by a trigger event, such as the 1989 Exxon *Valdez* oil spill in the case of the environment issue.

Notes

1. This case illustration is based on Kathryn Montgomery (1993, pp. 178-202) and Craig Reinarman (1988) as well as several personal discussions with Jay A. Winsten.
2. This case illustration draws on research conducted in San Francisco by the authors since 1986; see especially James W. Dearing and Everett M. Rogers (1992).
3. This case illustration is based on Conrad Smith (1993) and various other sources.
4. A *trigger event* is a cue-to-action that occurs at a point in time and serves to crystallize attention and action regarding an issue's salience.

3. Public Agenda Studies: The Hierarchy Approach

Apparently the average person takes the media's word for what the [issues] are, whether or not he personally has any involvement or interest in them.

G. Ray Funkhouser (1973b, p. 538)

To say that they set the agenda is to claim both too much and too little for the media of mass communication.

Gladys Engel Lang and
Kurt Lang (1981, p. 465)

The *public agenda* is the public's hierarchy of issues at a certain point in time. Two types of agenda-setting research have been conducted on the public agenda: (a) hierarchy studies, in which all of the main issues on the public agenda at a certain point in time are investigated, and (b) longitudinal studies, in which an agenda-setting scholar investigates the rise and fall of one or a few issues over time. These two types of research are quite different, and we treat them in separate chapters. The multiple-issue hierarchy studies are reviewed in this chapter, and the longitudinal studies of one or a few issues are analyzed in the following chapter.

Agenda-setting research got started with a hierarchy study. Maxwell McCombs and Donald Shaw (1972) gathered data about five main issues in their Chapel Hill study. It did not matter to these scholars exactly what the issues were in the 1968 presidential election. McCombs and Shaw wanted to explore the degree of isomorphism between the hierarchy of the five issues on the public agenda of their 100 undecided voters versus the relative amount of news coverage of these issues. In contrast, a longitudinal study of agenda-setting is usually driven by a scholar's interest in the over-time process of agenda-setting. Scholars who focus on a single issue typically ignore important information, such as the way in which the rise and fall of other issues may have affected the priority of the issue they are studying on the public agenda.

So, there are strengths and weaknesses of both the hierarchy and the longitudinal approaches to studying public agenda-setting.

The Issues of the 1960s[1]

At the same time that McCombs and Shaw (1972) were carrying out their classic agenda-setting study in Chapel Hill, G. Ray Funkhouser, a new PhD from Stanford University who was Assistant Professor of Communication at Pennsylvania State University, published an article reporting a quite different kind of agenda-setting study. Neither Funkhouser nor McCombs and Shaw were aware of each other's investigations until they presented both papers at the American Association for Public Opinion Research (AAPOR), the professional association of public opinion scholars. The two papers were both later published in AAPOR's journal, *Public Opinion Quarterly*.

How was Funkhouser's (1973a) issue-hierarchy approach to agenda-setting research different from McCombs and Shaw's (1972) Chapel Hill study? Like the North Carolina scholars, Funkhouser measured the multiple issues both on the media agenda and on the public agenda, and then correlated the priority of the issues on the two agendas. Unlike the North Carolina study, however, which dealt with the media agenda and the public agenda in one community, Funkhouser investigated these two agendas for the entire United States. He found the media agenda and the public agenda to be highly correlated, thus generalizing the McCombs-Shaw research results. This generalizability was a very important finding at the time. Naturally, Funkhouser's data were much more aggregated in nature than the McCombs-Shaw data.

Funkhouser (1973a) noted that in the 1960s, a number of new issues appeared on the national agenda, perhaps because of social unrest and protest. The rank order of the 14 issues studied by Funkhouser on the media agenda was indexed by the number of news articles in three weekly newsmagazines (*Time, Newsweek,* and *U.S. News*) as classified by the *Readers Guide to Periodical Literature*. The 14 issues were rank-ordered on the public agenda by Gallup Polls in which Americans were asked to name the most important problem facing the nation (Table 3.1).

Table 3.1 shows that the rank order of issues on the media agenda and on the public agenda were very highly correlated. This result confirms the McCombs and Shaw (1972) findings, generalizing them (a) from a single community to the nation and (b) from a several-month period in the 1968 presidential election to a decade.

Next, Funkhouser (1973a) analyzed the relationship of the media agenda and the public agenda on a year-by-year basis for eight issues for the period from 1964 to 1970 (when the most adequate data on the most important problem question were available). "The amount of media coverage for an issue during a given year is clearly related to whether or not it shows up as an important problem in the Gallup Poll" (Funkhouser, 1973a, p. 67). Note that Funkhouser was analyzing time as a variable in the agenda-setting process.

Finally, in a very important pioneering step in agenda-setting research, Funkhouser correlated the year-by-year media agenda for the 14 issues of the 1960s with real-world indicators for each issue. He was the first scholar to investigate the role of real-world indicators in agenda-setting. Funkhouser (1973a) found what most other scholars have discovered since: "The news media did

Table 3.1   The Rank Orders of the Media Agenda and the
Public Agenda in Ray Funkhouser's Study

Issue	Media Agenda (number of news articles)	Public Agenda (most important problem)
1. Vietnam War	1st	1st
2. Race relations and urban riots	2nd	2nd
3. Campus unrest	3rd	4th
4. Inflation	4th	5th
5. Television and mass media (including portrayals of violence, and other criticisms)	5th	12th (tie)
6. Crime	6th	3rd
7. Drugs	7th	9th
8. Environment and pollution	8th	6th
9. Smoking and health	9th	12th (tie)
10. Poverty	10th	7th
11. Sexual revolution	11th	8th
12. Women's rights	12th	12th (tie)
13. Science and society	13th	12th (tie)
14. Population growth	14th	12th (tie)

SOURCE: Funkhouser (1973a).

not give a very accurate picture of what was going on in the nation during the sixties" (p. 73). This general lack of a one-to-one relationship of media coverage with real-world indicators occurred (a) because of "artificial news," called "pseudo-events" by Boorstin (1961), in which news events such as civil rights demonstrations and Earth Day are staged to create news coverage of an issue, and (b) because an issue eventually ceased to be perceived as "news" after extensive media coverage. For instance, media coverage of the Vietnam War peaked in 1966, 2 years before the peak in the real-world indicator of the number of American troops in Vietnam (Figure 3.1). Newspeople, and the American public, may eventually have grown oblivious to claims of Vietcong body counts and television pictures of Vietnam villages being destroyed. Funkhouser (1973a) pointed out, however, that "these issues all had some basis in reality—that is, there was a war, the crime rate did rise, the value [of the dollar] did drop, and so forth" (p. 73).

44

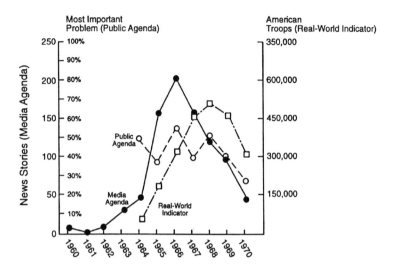

Figure 3.1. The Media Agenda, the Public Agenda, and a Real-World Indicator for the Issue of the Vietnam War in the 1960s

SOURCE: The data shown here are taken from Funkhouser (1973a, 1973b). Used by permission of the University of Chicago Press.

NOTE: The media agenda rises and falls ahead of the real-world indicator, while neither appears to be very highly related to the public agenda, on a year-by-year basis.

Previously, in Chapter 2, we discussed (a) the general lack of correspondence between the media agenda and real-world indicators and (b) how an issue rises in the agenda-setting process through a social construction of the issue by newspeople and by the public. Funkhouser could also have explored the relationship of the public agenda and real-world indicators, as we have done with his data (in Figure 3.1) for the issue of the Vietnam War.

Given that Funkhouser's study was so pioneering and so highly creative in its design, why isn't he, rather than Max McCombs and Donald Shaw, considered the founder of agenda-setting research? After all, here are two articles on the same new scientific topic, published in the same journal, appearing in almost the same year! Citations to these two journal articles by other scholars of agenda-setting are quite different (Table 3.2).

Table 3.2 The Number and Percentage of Citations to Two Classic
Articles by Other Agenda-Setting Scholars

Two Pioneering Publications on Agenda-Setting	Number of Citations
1. Funkhouser (1973a)	49 (24%)
2. McCombs and Shaw (1972)	115 (56%)

SOURCE: Rogers, Dearing, and Bregman (1993). Used by permission of Oxford University Press.

Why was Funkhouser's intellectual contribution so undervalued?

1. He did not label his research as dealing with the "agenda-setting" process, or cite publications in this tradition such as the Cohen (1963) metaphor ("The press tells us what to think *about*").[2]

2. Funkhouser's aggregated approach of using secondary data did not fit well with the personal interview survey methods then preferred by many mass communication scholars in investigating directional media effects. His study did not lead immediately to replications and to other types of follow-on research, as did the McCombs and Shaw piece.

3. Unlike Maxwell McCombs and Donald Shaw, Ray Funkhouser did not continue to conduct agenda-setting research himself or influence his students to do so. McCombs and Shaw wrote, co-wrote with each other, or cowrote with others a total of 32 publications on agenda-setting (about 9% of the total literature on this topic).

Measuring the Public Agenda

The public agenda is usually measured by means of a special kind of question in a public opinion poll. The usual public opinion poll asks for a respondent's attitude toward a particular issue. For example, a poll question might be, "How do you feel toward abortion?" or "What is your opinion about health care reform?" The special type of opinion poll question asked to index the public agenda usually takes the form: "What do you think is the most important problem facing this country today?" (Smith, 1980). This question (and minor variations of it) has been asked by the Gallup Poll some 200 times since World War II; it was first asked in a Gallup Poll back in 1935.

The MIP (most important problem) data show that five broad categories of national issues dominate the public agenda in the United States.

1. *Foreign affairs issues,* including war fears, military preparedness, and space, generally dominate the public agenda in the United States, averaging 40% to 50% of the MIP responses by the public from 1946 to 1976 (Smith, 1980).

2. *Economic issues* consist of inflation, unemployment, labor, and so on.

3. *Social control issues,* such as crime, violence, and moral decline, rose to importance in the late 1960s and early 1970s with race riots and campus unrest, and then continued at a modest level centered on fear of crime (Smith, 1980).

4. *Civil rights issues* became quite important in the mid-1960s but then were pushed down the public agenda by the Vietnam War.

5. *Government issues,* such as corruption, lack of leadership, and inefficiency, maintained a fairly low position on the national agenda, except at the time of the Watergate scandal·in 1974, when this category constituted 23% of the MIP responses (Neuman, 1990; Smith, 1980; Zhu, 1992a).

In addition to these five main issue categories, a specific issue such as health care or defense spending may rise to a high position on the public agenda for a brief period. But for most of the 20-year time period analyzed by Smith (1980), the four broad issues of foreign affairs, economic issues, social control, and civil rights topped the public agenda, with foreign affairs dominant. A time-series study of the public agenda over 40 years found that whereas the number of issues that constitute the American public's agenda has not changed, the substance of those issues has diversified, leading to a shorter average duration during which any one issue remains on the public agenda (McCombs & Zhu, 1995). These scholars conclude that more rapid turnover of issues on the public agenda may be evidence of a more segmented American society.

Gallup Poll data allow looking at differences in issue priorities by the characteristics of respondents. These differences in the MIP responses, however, are minor when compared with the issue priorities over time, which are mostly explained by historical events (e.g., the Vietnam War, Watergate, and the civil rights movement). Differences by type of respondent, when they do occur, are what one would expect. For example, black Americans and people living in the South ranked civil rights as an especially important problem facing the nation in the mid-1960s.

The MIP over the years has become the most widely used index of the public agenda at the national level. Even when agenda scholars are conducting their own interview survey of an audience to measure the public agenda in an issue-priority study, rather than using the Gallup Poll data, they frequently ask an MIP-type question. What are the advantages of the Gallup MIP as a measure of the public agenda? For one thing, the question does not suggest issue responses to the respondent, due to its open-ended nature. Imagine, in comparison, a set of closed-ended questions; for example, "How important is unemployment as an issue facing this country today? The environment? How about crime?" Obviously, one would have to ask a number of such questions, instead of just one, and there would always be the danger of overlooking some issue that might be on the public agenda. Further, closed-ended questions inevitably convey a high degree of suggestibility to respondents.

A further advantage of the MIP question is that it has been asked so consistently for so many years by the Gallup Poll that its future dominance for indexing the public agenda seems assured. Why change the wording of the question and lose comparability with the previous decades of MIP data?

There are several shortcomings of the MIP measure, however. For example, *facing America* are key words in the Gallup Poll question. As Funkhouser (1973a) noted:

> About the only way that people would estimate the most important problem *facing America* would be to take their cues from the media. The correspondence between news articles and public opinion . . . may be nothing more than the public's regurgitating back to the pollster what is currently in the news, with little or no relationship to what the respondent himself feels is important. (p. 69)

Thus, a positive relationship between the media agenda and the public agenda may be built into the MIP measure.

What if the public agenda were indexed by asking respondents, "What is the most important problem facing *you* today?" or, alternatively, "What is the most important problem that you feel our government should try to solve?" The answers are different from those obtained with the MIP question. For example, the Chapel Hill study asked,

"What are you *most* concerned about these days? That is, regardless of what the politicians say, what are the two or three *main* things which you think the government *should* concentrate on doing something about?" (McCombs & Shaw, 1972). *The public agenda depends to a large extent upon the way that it is conceptualized and measured* (Funkhouser, 1973b). This same cautionary statement, of course, can be made about every other dimension of public opinion.

Trumbo (1995) argues that if one conceptualizes an active media audience, then the typical agenda-setting perspective that issue salience and "thinking about" an issue are the same thing is misleading because deciding about the importance of an issue is inherently evaluative. In his longitudinal study of the issue of global warming, Trumbo (1995) conceptualizes and operationalizes an Extreme Concern Index (ECI) to measure the public agenda. Although the answers to MIP questions can readily be used for cross-sectional hierarchy studies, it is difficult to operationalize a longitudinal study using the public's answers to MIP questions because such answers will only exist for issues that have persisted as major issues for a long time. The ECI was created by gathering questions from two public opinion archives that (a) were about global warming, (b) were of national samples, (c) measured concern, and (d) used a scaled response to categorize respondent answers. So, unlike the MIP, the ECI is a combination of many different questions that are nevertheless rather similar. Trumbo (1995) found that the ECI correlated with the media agenda, which suggests that the index is a valid measure of public concern.

Most agenda-setting research has a "made in the United States" label (Chaffee & Izcaray, 1975). However, an invisible college of agenda researchers is developing in Japan. According to Takeshita (1993), since 1980, agenda-setting has become an indispensable subject in mass communication and political communication textbooks in Japan. An active group of investigators carries out agenda-setting research in Japan. Fortunately, for the advancement of the field, the Japanese approach to measuring the public agenda is somewhat distinctive. In addition to asking their version of the familiar MIP question in audience surveys,[3] the Japanese scholars also measure *perceived issue salience* (as did Weaver et al., 1981), defined as a respondent's perception of the salience of issues to a collectivity of other individuals.[4] In a 1993 Japanese replication of the 1968 Chapel Hill study, respondents were asked: "What do you think people in this city are most interested in, in this election?" In addition, *interpersonal issue salience*, the issues most frequently discussed in conversations with others, was measured by asking: "Did you discuss something about this election with your family or friends in the past week? If so, what kind of topics did you discuss and with whom?" (Takeshita, 1993).[5]

The MIP measure of the importance of the issues on the public agenda was not so highly correlated with the rank order of the issues on the media agenda (Spearman rho = .39) as was the perceived issue salience measure correlated with the media agenda (rho = .68). Takeshita (1993) concluded: "Mass media exert more influence on what people think about the climate of opinion than on what they think about as their own concerns." This conclusion supports the work of the German communication scholar Elisabeth Noelle-Neumann, who showed mass media coverage to have a powerful impact on what individuals think that other people are thinking. Presumably, people have little alternative to the media as a way of knowing others' concerns. One explanation for the superiority of perceived issue salience in Japan is that the Japanese have a strong need to know the climate of opinion of others about issue priorities. Such cultural differences in agenda-setting behavior need further exploration.

Evidence for the Influence of the Media Agenda on the Public Agenda

The major finding of the influential McCombs and Shaw (1972) study was that the issue hierarchy on the media agenda set the issue hierarchy of the public agenda. About two thirds of later studies (59 of the 92 empirical studies that we reviewed in 1992) confirmed this media agenda-public agenda relationship. Figure 3.2 depicts this directional relationship, along with the general finding that real-world indicators are less strongly related to either the media agenda or the public agenda.

A variety of research evidence supports the media-public agenda relationship:

1. Funkhouser's (1973a) investigation of issues in the 1960s, reviewed previously in this chapter, concluded that the public agenda is driven by the media agenda in the United States.

2. MacKuen's (1981) over-time study of the agenda-setting process for eight issues supports this generalization.

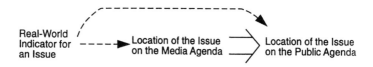

Figure 3.2. The Relationship Between Real-World Indicators of an Issue, Issue Position on the Media Agenda, and Issue Position on the Public Agenda

NOTE: The media agenda-public agenda relationship for an issue is not due to a high relationship of these two variables with a real-world indicator for the issue.

3. The laboratory experiments in which a media agenda is altered by the experimenter to test its effects on individuals' public agendas (Iyengar & Kinder, 1987) support this generalization.

4. Brosius and Kepplinger's (1990) over-time analysis of the agenda-setting process for 16 issues in Germany found support for the media agenda-public agenda relationship, even when the effects of these variables at a previous time period on themselves at a subsequent point in time were removed by Granger causality.[6]

So even when a variety of controls are taken into account in different types of designs and data analyses, the general conclusion of agenda-setting research is that *the media agenda sets the public agenda.* This is hardly surprising, but it represents support for a portion of our model of the agenda-setting process (depicted in Figure 1.1). Much of the variability in results of public agenda-setting research is due to a set of contingent conditions that importantly influence the media agenda-public agenda relationship. An overview and update of these conditions, expertly delineated by James Winter (1981), follows here.

Intervening Variables in Predicting the Public Agenda

The McCombs and Shaw (1972) Chapel Hill study aggregated the public agenda responses of their 100 respondents into one issue hierarchy (of five main issues). With a sample of only 100 respondents, there was no alternative to such aggregation. But in the several research studies retesting the main hypothesis of the Chapel Hill study, such as the McLeod et al. (1974) investigation in Madison, Wisconsin, and the Tipton et al. (1975) study in Lexington, Kentucky, data were gathered from larger samples, allowing these communication scholars to segment their respondents into various subaudiences on the basis of socioeconomic characteristics, personal experiences, and degree of media exposure.[7] Essentially, this type of research strategy was a disaggregation to determine if the media agenda-public agenda relationship found by McCombs and Shaw (1972) also held true for specific subaudiences. Generally, it did, although without strong and universal support.

An intervening variable in the media agenda-public agenda relationship is source or channel *credibility*, defined as the perception of a source/channel as trustworthy and competent. For example, a Wall Street lawyer may regard the *National Enquirer* as less credible regarding an international issue than the *International Herald-Tribune;* when the lawyer reads a headline in the *Herald-Tribune* about a new Palestine-Israel peace proposal, the medium's salience for this news item is more likely to be accepted (Rogers & Dearing, 1988). Several investigations (e.g., McCombs, 1977; Palmgreen & Clarke, 1977; Winter, 1981) sought to determine whether newspapers or television are more important in setting individuals' agendas. Wanta and Hu (1994) found that individuals who perceive the media as more credible relied on the media for information about issues in an Illinois election and were more susceptible to the media influencing their personal agenda of issues.

Further, the degree of media exposure by a sample of individuals is positively related to the degree to which they accept the media agenda as their personal agenda of issues. Research supporting this generalization includes Weaver, McCombs, and Spellman (1975), Shaw and Clemmer (1977), Mullins (1977), Einsiedel, Salomone, and Schneider (1984), and Wanta and Hu (1994).

The most widely studied intervening variable in explaining the media agenda-public agenda relationship is the amount of interpersonal discussion about an issue in the news. Does such interpersonal communication enhance or inhibit the agenda-setting effects of the mass media? "Few contingent conditions in agenda-setting have drawn so much attention from researchers with so little agreement in their results" (Wanta & Wu, 1992). By analyzing television and newspaper issue coverage for four weeks prior to conducting a random-digit-dial telephone survey of Illinois residents, Wanta and Wu concluded that interpersonal communication can reinforce public agenda-setting when such conversation concerns the same issues that the media had earlier emphasized. Interpersonal communication interrupts the media's agenda-setting influence when discussions concern other issues.

David H. Weaver at Indiana University has led in, among other things, explicating a *need for orientation* on the part of audience members to understand and control their informational environment. Individuals with high uncertainty will have a corresponding high need to become oriented about an issue. A high need for orientation will lead people to seek out more information in the mass media to reduce their uncertainty. This greater exposure to the mass media will then result in greater agenda-setting effects. Investigations supporting this generalization include Weaver (1977, 1984), Weaver et al. (1975), and Tipton et al. (1975).

The Role of Personal Experience With Issues

An individual's close familiarity with an issue, such as being unemployed or losing a close friend to cancer, is a way in which a person's personal experience with an issue overrides the influence of the mass media in determining what's important to that person. For most respondents, however, the media agenda predicts the issues that they rank as of highest salience. Some issues, by their very nature, are difficult or impossible for an individual to experience personally. Examples are the 1984 Ethiopian famine and the U.S. military presence in Somalia in 1992-1993. We learned almost all of our information about these issues either indirectly through the mass media, and especially television, or indirectly through interpersonal communication with others who also took their cues from the media (unless one had a friend or relative in the U.S. Armed Forces sent to Mogadishu).

Originally, Zucker (1978) found that "the less direct experience the people have with an issue . . . the greater is the news media's influence on public opinion on that issue" (p. 245). Support for this relationship is also provided by Manheim (1986) and Zhu, Watt, Snyder, Yan, and Jiang (1993). Presumably, individuals who lack personal experience with an issue must rely more on the mass media to set their public agenda. Thus, the media agenda is expected to be more important in setting the public agenda for international affairs than for domestic affairs.

On the other hand, personal experience with an issue can sensitize an individual to that issue, so that further information is then sought in the media about the issue. Thus, personal experience with an issue might enhance the media agenda's influence on the public agenda. When personal experience is indexed by the probability of being affected by an issue, a positive relationship of such personal experience with media agenda-setting was found (Erbring, Goldenberg, & Miller, 1980; Iyengar & Kinder, 1987).

Summary

In this chapter, we explored issue-hierarchy studies—investigations of all of the main issues on the public agenda at a certain point in time. The other type of public agenda-setting research (see our next chapter) investigates the rise and fall of a single issue (e.g., health care reform or international trade) on the public agenda over time or through experimental research with individuals.

Research evidence summarized in this chapter showed that often the media agenda sets the public agenda, although the empirical support for this relationship is far from overwhelming. A variety of types of public agenda-setting research support the media agenda-public agenda relationship: McCombs-Shaw-type cross-sectional investigations, over-time studies, and laboratory experiments in which actual newscasts are altered by splicing in additional television news coverage for an issue. The media agenda-public agenda relationship has usually been found even when various intervening variables (such as source/channel credibility and interpersonal discussion of the issue) are taken into account.

Notes

1. This case illustration is based mainly on G. Ray Funkhouser (1973a, 1973b).
2. Funkhouser, however, did cite the McCombs and Shaw (1972) paper in his second article (Funkhouser, 1973b), published in *Journalism Quarterly*.
3. Only 47% of Japanese respondents identified an issue in response to an MIP-type question.

4. This concept is similar to that measured by McLeod et al. (1974) as the degree to which an individual respondent talked about an issue with other members of the community, or other members raised the issue with the individual.

5. So few respondents identified an issue in response to this question that it could not be used to measure the public agenda.

6. Granger causality in the case of the agenda-setting process controls the influence of people's past public agenda on their present public agenda, so that the previous media agenda's effect on the people's current public agenda can be estimated independently of the people's past public agenda (Brosius & Kepplinger, 1990).

7. The Kentucky study also measured the media agenda and the public agenda at three points in time, so that the time order of the media agenda-public agenda could be determined with cross-lagged correlation techniques.

4. Public Agenda Studies: Longitudinal Approaches

Agenda-setting has not fully matured into a theory of media effects, yet this is part of its vitality. Agenda-setting is still on the path of inquiry and discovery. It has just arrived at the point where researchers are attempting to describe its natural history.

Craig Trumbo (1995, p. 2)

At the beginning of Chapter 3, we distinguished between hierarchy studies of (usually) six to eight issues versus longitudinal investigations of one or two issues in studies of public agenda-setting. Here we deal with longitudinal approaches to the study of the agenda-setting process that have become popular in very recent years. Longitudinal research, in which data from more than one point in time are collected, is well suited to investigating a *process*, which occurs over time. Longitudinal research designs represent one means of disaggregation in agenda-setting research, providing improved understanding of the process through which an issue comes to public attention, or of the psychological process through which individuals perceive issue salience.

One of the key assumptions of hierarchy approach agenda-setting studies is that the public—people who watch television, listen to the radio, and read the news—react to the mass media. For any one individual, that reaction is sometimes passive, sometimes active. The working hypothesis of the hierarchy approach is that the media's emphasis on certain issues and not other issues determines which issues we as members of the public think are important. This is a conception of a malleable, relatively passive U.S. public. David Weaver's conceptualization that people have a need for orientation (Weaver, 1977) was a means of bringing into agenda-setting research a theoretical rationale for those times when we are active seekers of information or entertainment. Other research strongly suggests that individuals engage in active psychological sense-making about public issues (Gamson, 1992; Liebes & Katz, 1990; Neuman et al., 1992) as well as active social activities that are intended to influence the outcomes of public issues (Blumer, 1971; Dearing & Rogers, 1992; Downs, 1972; Kingdon, 1984; Mead, 1994). For most issues, the majority of people are inattentive rather than attentive, and more passive than active. But for certain issues, depending on our own selective attention, we become very active and take charge of our information environment and, less frequently, organize for action. When this happens, hierarchy studies of agenda-setting do not show a deterministic media agenda-public agenda relationship (Neuman et al., 1992, pp. 110-112). In these circumstances, longitudinal studies of the agenda-setting *process* are more informative than hierarchy studies. Longitudinal designs better enable the researcher to operationalize active publics, which, it has been argued, is how public opinion really exerts itself on policymakers (Blumer, 1948).

The conceptualization of individuals being active information processors can also be extrapolated to society as a whole, as Frank Baumgartner and Bryan Jones (1993) did in their important book about policy agenda-setting, *Agendas and Instability in American Politics* (1993). They conducted longitudinal research on the issue of nuclear power and compared results with the issues of pesticides, tobacco, transportation safety, urban affairs, drug abuse, child abuse, and alcohol abuse. The collection and analysis of longitudinal data allowed Baumgartner and Jones (1993) to view society as an "issue processor" that functions to consider, debate, and sometimes institutionalize responses to conditions that we perceive as social problems.

The Issue of AIDS in the United States[1]

Our critique of agenda-setting research (Rogers & Dearing, 1988) recommended a strategy of disaggregation in future studies to unmask the human behavior change processes that are involved. Longitudinal agenda studies offer one means of disaggregation. We selected AIDS (acquired immunodeficiency syndrome) as a single issue to investigate. AIDS was a puzzling issue in an agenda-setting sense. Although the first AIDS cases were diagnosed in the United States in 1981, this issue did not attract much media attention until 4 years later, in mid-1985. By that time, more than 10,000 individuals had been diagnosed with AIDS, and about half that number had died. Why were the media so slow in discovering the issue of AIDS? What finally put AIDS on the agenda?

We measured the media agenda by the number of news stories about AIDS in the *New York Times*, the *Washington Post*, the *Los Angeles Times*, and the network evening newscasts of ABC, NBC, and CBS. From June 1981 through December 1988 (a period of 91 months), the six media of study carried 6,694 news stories about AIDS. Because media coverage of AIDS in each of the six media of study was highly intercorrelated across time, we combined the coverage by all six media into a variable indexing total mass media coverage of AIDS, which we used to measure the media agenda.

For the first 4 years of the epidemic, a point at which 9,944 individuals had AIDS, the issue was quite low on the mass media agenda (Figure 4.1). U.S. national mass media were slow to respond to the AIDS issue because of the lack of involvement of two traditional agenda-setting influences: the White House and the *New York Times*. As mentioned in earlier chapters, a U.S. president can move the media on any particular issue. President Reagan chose not to give a talk about AIDS until May 1987, 72 months into the epidemic, a point at which 35,121 AIDS cases had been reported by the CDC. The White House saw AIDS as a budget threat and so chose to ignore it.

The *New York Times* published its first page-one story about AIDS on May 25, 1983—12 months later than the *Los Angeles Times* and 10 months later than the *Washington Post*. The *New York Times's*

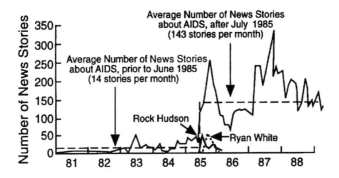

Figure 4.1. The Number of AIDS-Related News Articles in Six National Media of Study for 91 Months in the 1980s
SOURCE: Rogers et al. (1991). Used by permission of AEJMC.

management did not consider AIDS to be newsworthy from 1981 to mid-1985. Moreover, the newspaper's key medical writer broke his leg and was physically unable to cover breaking stories during this time. When a new executive editor was appointed in late 1985, coverage of AIDS expanded dramatically.

The number of news stories about AIDS escalated from an average of 14 per month prior to July 1985, to 143 per month after that date (see Figure 4.1). Conventional wisdom about the media coverage of AIDS credits this tenfold increase in news coverage to the July announcement that film actor Rock Hudson had AIDS. Our analysis shows that it was actually a concomitant news story of a young boy with AIDS, Ryan White, more than Hudson, that propelled AIDS up the media agenda. White was the topic of 117 news stories, while Hudson was the topic of 74. The White and Hudson disclosures together represent only 3% of our 6,694 news stories of study. The personification of the AIDS disease by White and Hudson changed the *meaning* of the issue for newspeople, who responded by giving more attention to AIDS. Several important AIDS news stories that broke earlier and that did *not* push AIDS up the media agenda are as follows:

58

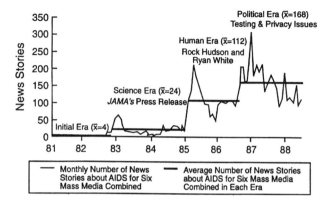

Figure 4.2. The Issue of AIDS Was Framed Differently in Each of the Four Eras of Media Coverage for This Issue
SOURCE: Rogers et al. (1991). Used by permission of AEJMC.

- The virus that causes AIDS was found in the blood supply, a news event announced in December 1982.
- Heterosexual contact as a means of HIV transmission was announced by the CDC in January 1983.
- Identification of the virus (HIV) that causes AIDS was announced in March 1984.
- A blood test for HIV antibodies was first reported in January 1985.

Even before July 1985, the rather limited AIDS coverage by the U.S. media had created a sharp increase in public awareness of the disease during 1983 and 1984, and had begun to correct the widespread misperceptions about methods of HIV transmission such as toilet seats and mosquito bites.

How was AIDS framed in the mass media? We identified four eras in the media coverage of AIDS: an Initial Era, a Science Era, a Human Era, and a Political Era. The Initial Era of AIDS media coverage was marked by only 59 news stories (Figure 4.2).

Media coverage during the second phase of 26 months through June 1985 depended on scientific sources. Of the 606 news stories in the Science Era, 40% were based on scientific sources.

The third phase of 19 months through January 1987, the Human Era, was characterized by personalizing the issue of AIDS. The Rock Hudson and Ryan White news events helped convince the U.S. public that AIDS was not just an epidemic among a unique category of people. These two events created the major turning point for the issue of AIDS on the U.S. media agenda.

The fourth phase of 23 months, February 1987 through December 1988, was a Political Era for the issue of AIDS. Public controversies emerged about certain aspects of the epidemic, especially public policy concerning mandatory testing and individual privacy. The government thus became deeply involved, and so AIDS became a political issue.

How did the issue of AIDS, once it rose on the U.S. mass media agenda in mid-1985, maintain such a prominent position in the face of competition from other important issues? The 6,694 news stories about AIDS were coded into 13 story themes, such as children with AIDS, public figures with AIDS, biomedical research findings, discrimination against individuals with AIDS, and so on. Analysis of the 13 AIDS themes shows that as any particular theme faded on the national agenda, another of the themes rose to take its place. How did the media, public, and policy agendas interact? The public agenda regarding the AIDS issue was measured by 110 national polls in which 1,084 questions regarding AIDS were asked of a total of 150,000 respondents. Two thirds of these polls were commissioned by mass media institutions. In this case, a "polling agenda" was set by the national media agenda (Dearing, 1989).

We also conceptualized a "science agenda" by operationalizing the number of articles about AIDS published in *Science*, the *Mortality & Morbidity Weekly Report* (the official journal of the U.S. Centers for Disease Control and Prevention), the *New England Journal of Medicine*, and the *Journal of the American Medical Association*. AIDS rose rapidly on the science agenda from 1981 through 1985 and then leveled off at 20 scientific articles per month.

Our analyses indicate that the real-world indicator of the severity of AIDS had very little impact on the other four agendas. The media agenda was affected by the science agenda, and to a less reliable extent by the polling agenda and the real-world indicator of the number of AIDS cases. The polling agenda was affected by both the media agenda and the policy agenda.

When interaction among the time-series data is analyzed for each of the four eras, the general model of the agenda-setting process (see Figure 1.1) is supported. During the Initial Era, the science agenda and the real-world indicator affected the media agenda. Many of the news stories were rewrites of science and medical journal press releases. During the Science Era, when scientific information about disease transmission dominated news content, the media agenda affected the polling agenda (pollsters asked questions in response to media coverage about AIDS). During the third stage, the Human Era, the media agenda and the polling agenda influenced each other. This relationship occurred because media organizations sponsored polls that asked questions about AIDS and then created news stories based on the poll results.

During the (fourth or) Political Era, both the science agenda and the media agenda influenced the policy agenda. The media agenda-policy agenda relationship during this fourth era contradicts the results from our full 91-month time-series analysis.

If the policy agenda is indexed by appropriations, in 1993, the federal government allotted $1.3 billion for AIDS research, $2 billion for cancer research, and $770 million for research on heart disease. Only 34,000 individuals died from AIDS in 1993, compared with 500,000 from cancer and 700,000 from heart disease. So, it is perceptions of health problems that influence policy decisions, not real-world indicators of mortality.

We conclude that studying agenda-setting over time, rather than cross-sectionally, can provide explanatory insights into the often intricate process of agenda-setting.[2]

The Issue-Attention Cycle

Two articles in the early 1970s popularized the over-time study, or "natural history" approach, to understanding the nature of social problems and public issues. In 1971, sociologist Herbert Blumer published an article that decried the reliance of many sociologists on cross-sectional and aggregated uses of quantitative data. Blumer emphasized the importance of studying the time-ordered stages of problems being recognized, then achieving legitimization as bona fide issues, their proponents and opponents organizing to push for resolution, and the possible outcomes of policy decisions.

In another much cited article 1 year later, political scientist Anthony Downs (1972) described what he called the "issue-attention cycle," the rise and fall of an issue on the public agenda. He noted: "Each of these problems [issues] suddenly leaps into prominence, remains there for a short time, and then—though still largely unresolved—gradually fades from the center of public attention." Downs (1972) postulated a series of stages in an issue-attention cycle:

(1) Pre-problem stage. Some undesirable situation (a social problem) exists but has not yet captured public attention. "Usually, objective conditions [real-world indicators] regarding the problem are far worse during the pre-problem stage than they are by the time the public becomes interested in it" (Downs, 1972).

(2) Alarmed discovery stage. A dramatic event suddenly creates public alarm about the issue, accompanied by euphoric enthusiasm about society's ability to solve the social problem.

(3) Realizing the cost of problem solution. At this stage, the public gradually realizes that the cost of solving the social problem is prohibitively expensive.

(4) Decline of public interest state. Now the issue begins to slip down the public agenda as interest fades, due to the high cost of solving the social problem and because the issue's extensive media coverage creates public boredom with the issue.

(5) Post-problem stage. The issue drops off of the public agenda, although the policies, programs, and organizations formed to cope with the social problem persist. For example, the EPA (Environmental Protection Agency), established during the first environmental crisis in the late 1960s, continues to the present day, although it was not very centrally involved in the environment issue in the early 1990s.

An issue's life cycle may indeed have discernible stages over time. Such longitudinal qualities could not be identified until scholars started conducting single-issue studies of the agenda-setting process. Whether these stages are very clear-cut, or whether stages differ for different issues, has yet to be determined by research.

How an Issue Gets on the Public Agenda

How do the mass media convey the priority of an issue to the public? Mainly through repetition, which cues the public as to the relative importance of an issue. The cumulative effect of media messages about an issue operates through the relentless, accumulated impact of a repeated message topic, which affects the public agenda. Previously, we suggested that national media give very similar coverage to issues on a month-by-month basis. The similarity in the amount of media coverage given to an issue creates a consensus about an issue's priority on the public agenda. It does not matter that one individual only reads the *Chicago Tribune* while another person only reads the *San Jose Mercury-News*; both newspapers eventually convey a similar priority for a national issue through their news coverage.

So, the media agenda influences the public agenda for an issue through a gradual and incremental process. As the cumulative number of media messages about an issue increases over time, the public becomes persuaded that the issue is important. Slowly, the public agenda for an issue builds up. Sometime later, it will melt away.

Experimental Research

One important type of agenda-setting research, begun in the 1980s, is experimental investigation of issue salience for individuals. These laboratory experiments artificially alter the media agenda (the experimental treatment) to test its effect on the public agenda of issues reported by individual subjects. The experimental approach to agenda-setting research was introduced by Shanto Iyengar, professor of communication and of political science at UCLA. In 1979, Iyengar began his association with Donald Kinder, a social psychologist at the University of Michigan. The first results of these experiments were published as a journal article in 1982 (Iyengar, Peters, & Kinder, 1982) and later as the book *News That Matters: Television and American Opinion* (Iyengar & Kinder, 1987). This volume is a celebrated classic, demonstrating the particular intellectual benefits that can be obtained from creatively using an alternate methodology, experimentation, to probe the psychology of the agenda-setting process, previously investigated only by survey-content analysis methods. The introduction of experimentation marked another methodological move toward disaggregation in agenda-setting research, and a focus on the micro-level behavior involved in the consequences of issue salience.

The experiments involved the investigators' active intervention in the agenda-setting process for individuals by altering the cues about issue salience. Videotapes of a television network's evening news broadcasts were doctored by inserting extra news coverage of some particular issue: civil rights, arms control, unemployment, and so on. Then, individuals were recruited to a university laboratory to view these doctored newscasts every day for a week (they were paid a small fee as an inducement to participate in the experiment). Other individuals were randomly assigned to watch a corresponding set of undoctored newscasts (thus serving as a control group). Both groups of respondents were asked about the salience of the manipulated issue (Iyengar & Kinder, 1985, p. 124). Respondents who had viewed the treatment videotapes, which contained extra news coverage of some issue, rated that issue as more important. Iyengar and Kinder (1987) carried out 14 different experiments along the general lines just described.

One consequence of such manipulation of individuals' issue hierarchy is *priming,* defined as the effects of a prior context on the interpretation and retrieval of information (Fiske & Taylor, 1984, p. 231). By lavishing news coverage on one issue while ignoring other issues, the mass media draw attention to certain aspects of political life at the expense of others (Iyengar & Kinder, 1987, p. 114). For instance, when people are primed by television news stories about the issue of national defense, people judge their president by how well they feel he has provided national defense. Certain issues in the United States are Republican Party issues (crime, for instance), while other issues such as poverty are Democratic Party issues. When the media elevate one or the other issue to higher saliency, they are inadvertently helping the political party that "owns" that issue. For instance, Iyengar and Kinder (1987) found that respondents who watched simulated television newscasts stressing the arms race cited this issue as a more important problem facing the nation. They also gave greater weight to President Reagan's performance on arms control and presumably would have been more likely to vote for Reagan in a presidential election. Whether subjects actually took this behavioral action was not measured.

Framing is the subtle selection of certain aspects of an issue by the media to make them more important and thus to emphasize a particular cause of some phenomenon (Iyengar, 1991, p. 11). Frames are one means through which a particular meaning is given to an issue. The laboratory experiments of agenda-setting provide improved understanding of how framing occurs, and of its consequences. These results about salience, priming, and framing suggest that the media agenda can do more than set the public agenda; it can also direct how individuals will evaluate issues (Entman, 1989; Iyengar, 1991; Salwen & Matera, 1992).

The Iyengar experiments on public agenda-setting have been followed up by several other scholars. For instance, an Iyengar-type experiment was conducted by Wolfgang Eichhorn (1993) in Germany, but instead of television, the front page of the local news section of a newspaper was altered to include extra material about (a) the growing crime problem in Munich or (b) how this city dealt with traffic problems. The respondents, who lived in Munich, regarded the issues on which they received extra coverage as more salient, thus supporting Iyengar and Kinder's results with television newscasts. Schoenbach and Semetko (1992) investigated the positive and negative tone of mass media coverage of the German national election on voters and concluded that the media's framing of an issue as positive or negative influenced the public's perceptions of issue salience.

A Threshold in Public Attention[3]

The media agenda-public agenda time sequence is not necessarily linear. Imagine a "critical mass" model in which some certain amount of media coverage of an issue must occur before the issue's salience on the public agenda is affected.

Russell Neuman (1990) investigated the Gallup Poll "MIP" measure of issue salience for 10 issues over the period from 1945 to 1980. The media agenda for these issues was operationalized by three media indexes: the *New York Times Index*, the *Readers Guide to Periodical Literature*, and the *Vanderbilt Television News Archive Index*.

Rather than simply correlating the media agenda with the public agenda, as many previous scholars had done, Neuman also looked at the relationships of these two variables when plotted against

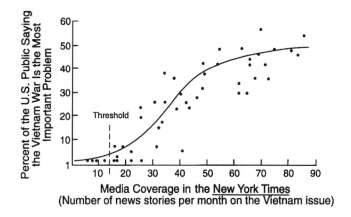

Figure 4.3. The S-Shaped Relationship of the Public Agenda With the Media Agenda for the Issue of the Vietnam War From 1962 to 1975
SOURCE: Neuman (1990). Used by permission of the University of Chicago Press.
NOTE: The position of the Vietnam War issue on the public agenda took off when about 15 news articles per month about the war were being published by the *New York Times*. The S-shaped public agenda response curve leveled off after 50 news stories per month on the war were being published.

each other over a time series. Figure 4.3 shows this type of analysis for the issue of the Vietnam War for the years from 1962 to 1975. The cumulative increase of media coverage of the Vietnam War eventually affected the public agenda for this issue. A threshold occurred in the *New York Times* media coverage when about 15 news articles per month were published. A critical mass of media salience was thus created, so that increases in the public agenda salience of the Vietnam War then took off. Eventually, the public agenda response leveled off (when about 50 news stories per month were published). Thereafter, the S-curve became a straight line.

A similar S-curve was found for 7 of the 10 issues of study, although the takeoff threshold was at a somewhat different point for each issue. For 2 of the 10 issues of study, the media agenda-public agenda relationship was linear; that is, a direct one-to-one relationship occurred without a takeoff (suggesting that a critical mass in media coverage did not affect the public agenda).

Issue Displacement as a Zero-Sum Game

"American public opinion rarely remains sharply focused upon any one domestic issue for very long—even if it involves a continuing problem of crucial importance to society," stated Anthony Downs (1972, p. 38). The public agenda is an ongoing process of competition among a relatively small number of major-issue proponents. When respondents in national surveys are asked to name as many issues as they wish, they average only four or five issues (Brosius & Kepplinger, 1992b). If the public agenda contains only a limited number of issues at any given time, the agenda-setting process must, theoretically, be a zero-sum game. In other words, if an issue is to climb the public agenda, it must push other issues down the agenda and eventually shove one of the earlier issues off of the agenda.

Relatively few studies have investigated this evolutionary process by looking at the rise and fall of various issues over time. One exception is a study by Zhu (1992a) of three issues: the federal budget deficit, the Persian Gulf War, and the economic recession in the United States. From June 1990 to April 1991, an 11-month period, these three issues together accounted for 40% of all the responses in national polls when respondents were asked to name the most important problem (MIP) facing the country. The three issues of study "fought" each other for this portion of the public agenda: When Iraq invaded Kuwait (in early August 1990), the Persian Gulf issue pushed the federal deficit issue down the agenda. But in October 1990, the federal government fiscally shut down for a few days, and news stories about the budget deficit dominated. Then, in December 1990, the military buildup in the Gulf became the main news item, and concern about the approaching Gulf War pushed the federal deficit issue down the public agenda. The rise of one issue clearly occurred at the expense of another issue. Media agenda-setting attracted the public audience for an issue away from competing issues (Zhu, 1992a).

Evidence that the public agenda is a zero-sum game is also provided by the Gallup MIP polls, in which national samples of the U.S. population are asked: "What do you think is the most important problem facing this country today?" These MIP polls, described in the previous chapter, show that about five issues are on the national agenda at any point in time, at least if one requires a minimum of 10% of the respondents to say that a particular issue is the MIP facing the nation. Rather amazingly, the *same* five broad issues have been on the national agenda since Gallup began asking the MIP question decades ago (Smith, 1980). These most-noted issues are foreign affairs, the nation's economic situation (including inflation and employment), social control issues (such as law and order), civil rights, and government. In most cases, if a specific issue does not fit into one of these broader issue categories, it does not climb the public agenda.

To investigate whether a new issue must necessarily displace another issue on the media agenda, James Hertog, John Finnegan, and Emily Kahn (1994) combined a test of Zhu's zero-sum suggestion with a theoretical model developed by Stephen Hilgartner and Charles Bosk (1988), who built on Blumer's (1971) stage model of social problem development. Using Hilgartner and Bosk's idea that social problems "compete," especially with *similar* problems, Hertog et al. (1994) studied the over-time rise and fall of stories about AIDS, cancer, and sexually transmitted diseases other than HIV (the AIDS virus). Their results across different types of mass media suggest little evidence that these issues exhibited a zero-sum relationship on the media agenda. At least for some related issues, displacement does not occur.

Time in Agenda-Setting Research

The original empirical studies such as the McCombs and Shaw (1972) investigation in Chapel Hill were "timeless" in that they consisted of a cross-sectional analysis of data gathered at one point in time. However, both the Cohen (1963) metaphor and the McCombs-Shaw paradigm clearly implied that agenda-setting was a process over time. Eventually, the time dimension was brought into agenda-setting research. Methods of investigating the process aspects of agenda-setting include moving from issue-hierarchy studies to investigations of a single issue.

When real-world indicators, the media agenda, and other agenda variables are measured over time, such as on a month-by-month basis, time-series data analysis methods can be used to understand the time order of these variables. The expected time order for the four main variables in the agenda-setting process are shown in Figure 4.4.

A time sequence like the one shown generally occurs in the agenda-setting process. For instance, MacKuen (1981) found that for six of his eight issues of study, the media agenda led the public agenda. The

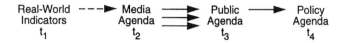

Figure 4.4. The Expected Time Order of Real-World Indicators, the Media Agenda, the Public Agenda, and the Policy Agenda, With the Degree of Evidence for Each of These Expected Relationships
NOTE: The strongest evidence for the expected time order of these four variables in the agenda-setting process is for the media agenda-public agenda relationship. Further research is needed to determine the actual time order for the other relationships.

average time lag was several months. Other investigations have also found a time lag, from a few weeks to several months, between the media agenda and the public agenda (Rogers et al., 1991; Shoemaker, et al., 1981). The length of this period depends upon such factors as the nature of the issue, its amount of media coverage, and so forth (Eyal, 1979; Eyal et al., 1981; Mazur, 1981, 1987).

Christine Ader (1993) correlated the media agenda for the issue of the environment, measured 3 months before a public opinion poll about the salience of this issue, with the poll's MIP percentage, and also correlated the media agenda, measured 3 months after each poll, with the poll's MIP percentage. For 66 Gallup MIP polls, the correlation of the pre-poll media agenda with the public agenda is $r = .224$, while the post-poll media agenda is correlated $r = .165$ with the public agenda. The first correlation is larger and explains about twice as much variance as the second, leading Ader (1993) to conclude that the media agenda precedes the public agenda in time order. This conclusion supports our model of the agenda-setting process (see Figure 1.1 in Chapter 1).

In addition to the expectation that the media agenda should lead the public agenda, we expect (a) that a real-world indicator should lead the media agenda, and (b) that the public agenda should lead the policy agenda, but these time-ordered relationships have not been explored in many studies.

Quantitative data analyses of the relationships among variables over time are not the only method for determining time order in the agenda-setting process. By arranging the key events that occur for an issue in their actual time sequence, a scholar may be able to understand certain processual aspects of the agenda-setting process.[4] This interpretive pro-cess can complement a statistical time-series analysis.

How the Ethiopian Famine
Got on the Agenda[5]

The histories of how issues get on the national agenda provide a general picture of accident, fortuitous events, and chance happenings, along with rare instances of media advocacy. Certainly, for each of the dozen or so major issues that get on the national agenda in any given year, there are hundreds and perhaps thousands of other issues that do *not* get on the agenda. The agenda-setting process is like a gigantic funnel with many, many candidate issues entering the wide mouth but very few issues surviving to get on the national agenda. Exactly what happens in this funneling process?

One answer is provided by the way the Ethiopian famine got on the U.S. agenda (and the international agenda) in October 1984, and how the Brazilian drought, which was much more serious by any objective measure, did *not* get on the U.S. agenda. Back in early 1984, these two drought-plagued countries were hard hit by starvation. In Ethiopia, more than 6 million people were trekking to government feeding stations. In Northeast Brazil, 24 million people were facing the worst drought in 200 years. International food relief agencies such as the British-based charity Oxfam saw the two problems of Ethiopia and Brazil as roughly comparable (Boot, 1985). Why did the Ethiopian famine get on the agenda but not the Brazilian disaster?

Ethiopia became one of the major news stories of the year in 1984 because it attracted television reporters whose broadcasts led to immense donations for food relief from the public. In Brazil, meanwhile, starvation quietly continued. In this instance, the media agenda-setting process had vital consequences. "Fate is the editor" (Boot, 1985). The nature of the Brazilian famine did not fit with "good television": Government feeding stations were scattered over a vast territory, rather than being crowded together, as in Ethiopia, where dying children were concentrated in places that were convenient for television camera persons. "If there's no picture, there's no story" (Boot, 1985).

Actually, pictures about the Ethiopian famine were available for many months before the story "broke" in October 1984, but the media initially failed to react. Key gatekeepers said: "Ho-hum. Starving children in Africa? What's newsworthy about that?" By midsummer, an estimated 7,000 Ethiopians were dying each month. The media dam finally broke in late October, when Mohammed Amin, a Visnews cameraman, paired with BBC correspondent Michael Buerk to file a report from Northern Ethiopia, focusing on a refugee camp at Korem. "As viewers saw a three-year-old child die on camera and a throng of adults resembling Auschwitz inmates, Buerk narrated: 'Death is all around. A child or adult dies every twenty minutes' " (Boot, 1985, p. 47). The BBC broadcast the Ethiopian video report on October 23, 1984. The audience response in England was immediate. Phone calls flooded the BBC as individuals offered donations.

NBC's bureau in London conveyed the Amin-Buerk news report on the Ethiopian drought to New York by satellite, urging that it be broadcast in the United States that evening. October 23 was just a few weeks before the November presidential election, and the NBC evening news broadcast was already packed with political stories. But when NBC anchorman Tom Brokaw saw the stunning film footage from Ethiopia, he ruled that it had to be included in that evening's news show. A 3½-minute segment was broadcast. Telephones at the headquarters of Save the Children, which Brokaw had mentioned on the air, began ringing off the hook. Massive news coverage of the Ethiopian famine followed immediately in the *New York Times*, the *Washington Post*, and other national news media. NBC, CBS, and ABC quickly dispatched film crews to Ethiopia. Soon thereafter, rock musicians organized benefit activities to raise tens of millions of dollars of food aid. U.S. government and international agencies quickly joined the relief efforts. In Brazil, meanwhile, the famine continued without international fanfare.

Ten months later, after mid-1985, the Ethiopian famine quietly slipped back down the U.S. media agenda (see Figure 2.1 in Chapter 2). The starvation continued, but media attention turned elsewhere, except for an occasional news article over the next several years.

Summary

This chapter dealt with the public agenda-setting research that uses a single-issue approach, a perspective that has emerged in recent years as one important means of disaggregation. The research paradigm assumes an active, involved public, as opposed to the hierarchy approach, which assumes a passive role for audience members, that of adopting media salience for issues. One main advantage of the single-issue approach is that the agenda-setting process can be traced longitudinally to better understand the time sequence in which the media agenda, public agenda, and policy agenda occur.

This expected sequence, postulated by Blumer (1971) and Downs (1972), has been shown to have generally occurred in a small number of empirical studies. Thus, we see evidence from several studies that media agenda-setting is a process of social construction. Key individuals gradually give meaning to an issue through interaction with each other. Perceptions, not real-world indicators, count.

Priming is the effect of a prior context on the interpretation and retrieval of information. Thus, when news coverage of an issue gives that issue salience with the public, people may be more likely to support a political leader who is identified with the issue. *Framing* is the subtle selection of certain aspects of an issue by the media to make them more important and thus to emphasize a particular cause of some phenomena.

Notes

1. This case illustration is based mainly on Everett M. Rogers, James W. Dearing, and Soonbum Chang (1991).

2. Trumbo (1995) investigated the single issue of global warming during the 1980s and early 1990s, using a similar time-series analysis to the study reported here.

3. This case illustration is based mainly on W. Russell Neuman (1990).

4. Examples of such time ordering of key elements in the agenda-setting process for an issue are Walker (1977) and Rogers et al. (1991).

5. This case illustration is based on William Boot (1985) along with other sources.

5. Policy Agenda Studies

The great problem in American politics is: What makes things happen?

E. E. Schattschneider (1960, p. vii)

Agendas are not first set and then alternatives generated; instead, alternatives must be advocated for a long period before a short-run opportunity presents itself on an agenda.

John W. Kingdon (1984, p. 215)

The central topic of this chapter is how an issue gets on the policy agenda, and leads, perhaps, to government policies designed to address or solve a social problem. A public policy may be expressed in the form of a new law, an executive order, an appropriation, or some other governmental action. The policy agenda is of key importance because it represents an outcome of activity and influence on the media agenda and on the public agenda. For the mass, inattentive public, public policies represent the resolution of problems that were issues on the public agenda. In practice, however, public policies often function not to solve difficult societal problems but to institutionalize a response to those problems. The policy institutionalization of responses to public issues is how governments grow (Baumgartner & Jones, 1993).

Policy agenda-setting is not typically of central concern to communication scholars, but many researchers who have recognized the critical societal roles of communication have been centrally concerned with policy agenda-setting. Walter Lippmann, Robert Park, Gabriel Almond, James Davis, James Rosenau, and Bernard Cohen, the forerunners of agenda-setting research, directed their attention to policy agenda-setting as well as to the particular role of the mass media. Contemporary mass communication scholars such as Maxwell McCombs, Donald Shaw, and Shanto Iyengar have a keen interest in political outcomes, expressed in their research as the likelihood to vote, the voting preference of subjects, or the manipulation of advertising by political candidates.

Policy agenda-setting has been of somewhat less interest to communication scholars than the subprocesses of media agenda-setting and public agenda-setting because policy agenda-setting involves collective political behavior as well as communication behavior. As conceptualized and operationalized by sociologists who study social movements and political scientists who study decision making, policy agenda-setting is more complex than either media or public agenda-setting. The public and the mass media are just two types of influences on policy agendas; yet they are important influences. For example, a wide-ranging and sophisticated analysis of more than 142,000 telephone survey responses over 12 years tested the relationship between public opinion and policy making in each of the 50 states. The authors concluded that "public opinion is the dominant influence on policy making in the American states" (Erikson, Wright, & McIver, 1993, p. 244). But how does that influence actually occur?

Scholars investigating policy agendas have concentrated on how a political issue gets on the agenda of a city, state, or national government. Often, a case study approach is followed in an attempt to reconstruct the main events and decisions in the process of policy determination. Barbara Nelson's (1984) book, *Making an Issue of Child Abuse: Political Agenda Setting for Social Problems*, is an example of reconstructing the variety of forces that gave rise to a state and national issue. On a local level, Timothy Mead (1994) conducted a case study of the *Charlotte Observer* newspaper and its editors' attempts to put the issue of metropolitan reform on the local policy agenda. By using archives, personal interviews, and his own experience, Mead tells the intricate story of how even though the newspaper has failed in its objective of consolidating city and county governments, the *Observer* has been successful in repeatedly getting the problem of government inefficiency placed as an issue on the policy agenda. Mead (1994) uses Kingdon's (1984) model to explain the newspaper's influence in pushing its concerns up the policy agenda, of working on opponents and decision makers to "soften them up," and of reframing the issue of metropolitan reform so that it comes to be perceived as related to other desirable goals, such as accountability and leadership. In this case, a mass media organization is clearly an issue proponent: "We bring it [consolidation] up at every opportunity. Any time anyone mentions it, we report it. And if they don't mention it, we say they should have" (Williams, 1993, quoted in Mead, 1984, p. 35).

The Media-Policy Relationship

Policymakers are expected to consume themselves with issues that represent our most dogged social problems. For the U.S. media, especially, the careful analysis of problems, the application of various interventions (such as the federal Head Start program), and their evaluation and possible reauthorization just does not make for good news. It is too slow, too gradual, and too issue centered. American journalism values newness above all else and is thus biased toward events, not drawn-out issues (Jamieson, 1992; Patterson, 1993). This is one reason for the media agenda's less than constant influence on the policy agenda (Kingdon, 1984, p. 62). So, although policymakers pay close attention to and are often forced to respond to media coverage, and reporters prize their access to elected officials as story sources, the media-policy relationship is defined by this temporal disjuncture of reporters needing immediacy to do their jobs and policymakers needing contemplation to do their jobs. The relationship of media reporters and policymakers is symbiotic in that journalists need access to the sources of news and policymakers need coverage of their proposals and actions; nevertheless, the needs of journalists and policymakers are often incompatible because of their different orientation to time.

The mass media often have a direct influence on the policy agenda-setting process, in addition to their indirect influence through the public agenda-setting process (see Figure 1.1). For example, Kingdon (1984) found that a window of opportunity for addressing or solving a social problem occurs (a) when a problem (b) converges with a solution in search of a problem (c) in a favorable political climate. Kingdon (1984) applied a model of decision making in organizations (Cohen, March, & Olsen, 1972) to public policy making. He concluded that the relationship of problems, policies, and politics in the decision-making process is not random; it is opportunistic. Kingdon usefully distinguished the agenda-setting process from the process of alternative specification. He considered agenda-setting to be a narrowing of the set of subjects that could occupy policy attention to the list on which attention is actually focused. *Alternative specification* is the process of narrowing the range of possible positions for any one issue. Scholars of public agenda-setting would label this process *media framing*.

Policymakers regularly use the media to accomplish their goals. There is little doubt that circularity better defines the total agenda-setting process (Figure 1.1) than does a linear and directional media-public policy model. Kingdon (1984), Linsky (1986), Rogers and Dearing (1988), Baumgartner and Jones (1993), and Trumbo (1995), among others, argue for circular models of the agenda-setting process that include certain general directional relationships (such as media to public). Even those scholars who present their ideas as stage models, such as Blumer (1971), Downs (1972), and Nelson (1984), include recursive feedback loops.

Recursivity means that the policy agenda, for example, has influence on the public agenda and public behavior. Derksen and Gartrell (1993) demonstrate the importance of conceptualizing and operationalizing recursivity in a study of the social context of recycling behavior in Canada. People who had curbside recycling in their community (a public policy in place) and who had pro-environmental attitudes engaged in recycling behaviors. People who did not have curbside recycling in their community (no policy enacted), even those who had pro-environmental attitudes, tended not to recycle.

Previously, for example, we stated that the U.S. president can put an issue on the national agenda just by giving a talk about it. If the president does not do so, the issue is hampered in its likelihood for getting on the agenda. The U.S. president "is the political system's thermostat, capable of heating up or cooling down the politics of any single issue or of an entire platter of issues" (Bosso, 1987, p. 261). A thermostat exerts powerful influence in a system: "No other single actor in the political system has quite the capability of the president to set agendas in given policy areas for all those who deal with these policies" (Kingdon, 1984, p. 17). Yet, of course, a U.S. president can ignore an issue and it can still get on the media and public agendas. This is a politically dangerous position for an elected official such as a president, as well as for government agency bureaucrats, who then risk losing control over how the issue is defined and framed on both agendas. For example, there are many cases in which the U.S. Environmental Protection Agency and the Department of Energy tried to hide information about the siting of waste treatment facilities or soil and water contamination problems. In hindsight, the bureaucrats involved would have fared far better in the public spotlight of media attention if they had proactively released information and sought to portray their problems and activities to their advantage before journalists or issue opponents such as consumer interest groups and environmental organizations defined and framed the issues. How an issue is reported is as important as whether the issue is reported at all.

Given that the U.S. president is a dominant force in setting the national agenda, how is the president's agenda set? Certain issues enter the White House with the election of a president, perhaps because they were a campaign promise (an example was President Bill Clinton's health care issue). Other issues are championed by a president after they bubble up through the media agenda and the public agenda, perhaps originally instigated by trigger events over which the president has no control but to which he must respond. Finally, certain issues are placed on the national agenda by the power of world events, such as a warlike act by some foreign power or by an international disaster, whether the president likes it or not. The mass media are omnipresent and central in the world of policy making (Linsky, 1986). Cohen (1965) described the central role of the media in foreign policy making:

> The press functions in the political process like the bloodstream in the human body, enabling the [foreign policy] process that we are familiar with today to continue on, by linking up all the widely-scattered parts, putting them in touch with one another, and supplying them with political and intellectual nourishment. (p. 196)

Media Coverage and Decision Making in Washington[1]

What goes on inside the Washington Beltway is puzzling to most Americans, but they would generally agree that the mass media are important influences in federal policy making. Evidence for the degree of media influence is provided by Martin Linsky, a lecturer in the John F. Kennedy School of Government at Harvard University. Linsky was uniquely qualified to lead a study of mass media influence on federal policy making. He had been a three-term member of the Massachusetts House of Representatives and assistant attorney general for the Commonwealth of Massachusetts as well as an editorial writer and reporter for the *Boston Globe*. Linsky's team of researchers investigated the role of the mass media by conducting six case studies. Their topics were the 1969 reorganization of the Postal Department, the resignation of Vice President Spiro T. Agnew, the decision of President Jimmy Carter not to deploy the neutron bomb, the relocation of 700 families from the Love Canal area in New York State, the Reagan administration's support of a tax exemption for Bob Jones University, and the 1984 suspension of Social Security Disability reviews.

These six case studies show that Washington policymakers often infer the public agenda from the media agenda (Linsky, 1986; Linsky, Moore, O'Donnell, & Whitman, 1986). That is, government officials and politicians take the amount of media attention given to an issue as an indirect expression of public interest in the issue. This inference is not as strange as it might seem, as we know that the media agenda is related to the public agenda. The bureaucrats and elected leaders in Washington, D.C., could better consult poll data (such as the MIP) to track an issue on the public agenda. But they often don't.

Second, Linsky (1986) shows that many political factors, such as political party differences, the role of lobbying organizations, and the personal power of individual politicians are involved in determining the policy agenda. But for the mass media, he reserves an especially crucial role. In Linsky's (1986) cases, media coverage affects the ability of policymakers to get their policies successfully adopted and implemented. Many politicians and powerful bureaucrats learn of each other's activities through the mass media. So policymakers attempt to get positive coverage for their issues while tipping off reporters about negative aspects of competing issues. In short, policymakers proactively use the media to further their own policy goals. Many of the senior officials whom Linsky interviewed said that the media had a larger impact on the *process* of policy making (such as timing and the extent of consultation before making a decision) rather than the *content* of the policies themselves. And these same officials are frustrated by the media's ability to affect their issue priorities. In keeping with Kingdon's (1984) adaptation of Cohen et al.'s (1972) "garbage can model of organizational choice," which views federal policy making as an organized anarchy of problems, policies, and politics, Linsky (1986) found that policy agenda-setting is

> not subject to rigid rules or formulae. It is the result of the interplay of various currents, including but not limited to the intent of both journalists and officials. Journalists can set the agenda without trying, just by doing their jobs. (p. 89)

From the Issue of Power to the Power of Issues

Power is the crucial concept of study for many political scientists and international relations scholars, dating from Hans J. Morgenthau's classic book *Politics Among Nations* (1948). Because setting the policy agenda involves the use of individual and organizational power, it attracts the attention of contemporary political scientists, historians, and sociologists who are concerned with the actual or potential use of power.

One of the most influential studies in the policy agenda research tradition was by Roger W. Cobb and Charles D. Elder (1972/1983), *Participation in American Politics: The Dynamics of Agenda-Building.* Published at about the same time as the McCombs and Shaw (1972) Chapel Hill study, the Cobb and Elder book similarly laid out many of the basic concepts for the policy agenda-setting investigators who followed. For example, Cobb and Elder (1972/1983, p. 85) emphasized the role of trigger events in issue creation. A *trigger event* is a cue-to-action that occurs at a point in time and serves to crystallize attention and action. In earlier chapters, we encountered numerous examples of trigger devices: the 1986 death of Len Bias and the War on Drugs; the 1989 Exxon *Valdez* oil spill and the environmental issue; and the 3½-minute television film broadcast by NBC on October 23, 1984, of the Ethiopian famine. Such triggers help the mass media frame an issue and also help the issue catch the public's attention. Essentially, a trigger event simplifies the nature of a complex issue into a form that the public can more easily understand. The public faces many issues at any point in time, far more than they can understand completely, given their limited time and attention. Thus, a trigger is a propelling force that helps an issue climb the agenda.

How is the study of policy agenda-setting different from other research by political scientists? Both types of scholars center their attention on the study of power, but policy agenda scholars focus on the power of issues, a much more specific research topic than the issue of power (Mansbach & Vasquez, 1981). Also, scholars of policy agenda-setting use research methods that allow them to follow issues over time and incorporate the analysis of many difficult-to-quantify variables, such as leader personality and control over how issues are framed.

Due to their different goals of seeking to explain the behavior of nations, international relations scholars have categorized issues in different ways than have scholars of public agenda-setting. A series of deductive issue typologies have been proposed. For example, Lowi

(1964) distinguished between *distributive issues,* which do not involve much expenditure of public funds and do not generate much interest from public groups; *regulatory issues,* which involve the allocation of contested public funds, and combative public interest groups, and so result in winners and losers; and *redistributive issues,* which encourage political leaders to divide public funds for problem solution in many ways in an attempt to pacify all of the involved attentive public groups. Rosenau (1971) proposed a division of issues according to the status of each issue, the extent to which human and nonhuman resources are required, the territory affected, and the extent to which the means and ends of issue resolution are tangible. Zimmerman (1973) extended Lowi's (1964) typology to foreign policy issues. Brecher, Steinberg, and Stein (1969), in a substantive typology more similar to those of mass communication scholars, considered issues to be military-security, political-diplomatic, economic, or cultural. Empirical tests of these issue typologies provide the most support for the Rosenau typology (Mansbach & Vasquez, 1981, pp. 36-47). Mansbach and Vasquez (1981), building on Cobb and Elder (1972/1983), propose a model of how and why issues get on the global policy agenda by focusing on issue proponents, issue salience, what is at stake, the nature of the stake, and the values associated with the stakes at hand. Baumgartner and Jones (1993) build on many of these ideas in their development of a methodology for combining cross-sectional and longitudinal approaches to the study of policy agenda-setting.

Investigative Reporting and Policy Making in Chicago[2]

Investigative reporting of the Watergate incident by two *Washington Post* newspeople, Woodward and Bernstein, contributed to the resignation of a U.S. president in 1974. The purpose of investigative reporting is to bring about a policy change, so it is intimately related to the agenda-setting process. Basically, the results of investigative reporting, when they appear in the mass media, ought to lead to a policy change. Whether they do so or not is an important topic of research for communication scholars and for students of policy making.

A decade ago, a band of scholars in Northwestern University's Center for Urban Affairs planned a research program on the role of investigative reporting in the policy agenda-setting process. This interdisciplinary research group was led by David Protess, a professor in the Medill School of Journalism at Northwestern, and included several scholars who had worked as investigative reporters. Despite the important role of investigative reporting in American journalism, little scholarly research had been conducted on whether or not investigative journalism actually results in policy change.

The Northwestern University research team designed a series of six field experiments on the effects of investigative reporting about the issues of government fraud and abuse in a health care program, rape, toxic waste disposal, international child abductions, police brutality, and unsanitary conditions and fraud at federally funded kidney dialysis centers. The scholars would learn well in advance that an exposé resulting from investigative reporting was about to appear in the media. About 2 weeks before this news event, the Northwestern University scholars gathered survey data (a) from a sample of audience members and (b) from a small sample of policymakers. Then, several weeks after the results of the investigative reporting were announced publicly, the scholars reinterviewed these same respondents to determine the effects of the investigative news reports on the public agenda and on the policy agenda. To conduct these field experiments with their limited resources, Protess and his colleagues studied investigative reporting's impacts in the Chicago and Philadelphia areas. Most other agenda scholars have not been able to use field experimental designs because they do not know in advance when media coverage of a new issue will occur. Use of this research design was a major advance by the Protess team. For scholarly research purposes, one of the important aspects of investigative reporting is that it is planned and thus can be anticipated by field experimenters.

One of the six field experiments, which dealt with investigative reporting on the issue of rape in Chicago, illustrates the research approach used by Protess and his Northwestern University colleagues (Protess, Leff, Brooks, & Gordon, 1985). This field experiment used a pre- and postmeasure design to determine the effects of a newspaper investigative series about rape (a) on a random sample of 347 Chicago residents and (b) on a purposive sample of 39 policymakers. The investigative reporting was carried out by the *Chicago Sun-Times* newspaper and dealt with government improprieties in handling rape cases. Local police departments, especially in suburban areas, were intentionally underreporting rape cases, and state and local officials were not taking adequate measures to punish the offenders.

What effects did this weeklong series of newspaper stories, titled "Rape: Every Woman's Nightmare," have on the media, public, and policy agendas in Chicago? Very little measurable effect on the public agenda, and not much on policymakers, Protess and others (1985) found. Policymakers were already concerned about rape and responded to the newspaper series mainly by announcing various symbolic actions that had little actual substance. For instance, the Chicago mayor announced the establishment of a Rape Hotline, which had actually been created months earlier. The main effects of the investigative reporting about rape were on the media agenda itself. The *Sun-Times* gave much more attention to the issue of rape over the several months following publication of the series of investigative articles on rape in Chicago.

Taken together, the six cases studied by David Protess and his colleagues (1991) suggested to them that a direct public agenda influence on the policy agenda can occur, but the relationship is "weak and unreliable" (p. 19). They documented policy decisions being made in the absence of public reaction. And an issue's rise on the local policy agenda was often the result of behind-the-scenes collaboration between investigative journalists and city officials. When these scholars did see evidence of the public agenda at work, it was not in evidence through the use of random selection public opinion polls but through organized and special interest groups.

Studying the Policy Agenda

Compared with research about the media agenda-public agenda link, investigations of policy agenda-setting have been fewer in number, and this research front has been less coherent. Even though the number of empirical studies of policy agenda-setting is small, a diversity of approaches have been attempted.

Field experiments like the Northwestern University studies of investigative reporting can provide insight into the causal factors involved in the agenda-setting process. David Protess and his research team at Northwestern University studied the consequences on the policy agenda of a particular type of mass media content, investigative journalism. They conceptualized an "investigative agenda" and related it to local public opinion and policy agendas.

A quite different and more typical approach, exemplified by the six case studies of policies carried out by Martin Linsky and his colleagues, is to begin with a public policy that has been enacted and then trace it retrospectively through the agenda-setting process. Jack Walker's (1977) study of the passage of the 1966 Traffic Safety Act is also an example of this backward-tracing approach.

Does the policy agenda-setting process actually lead to changes in behavior, and to solution of the original social problem, or, with time, does the problem just go away? In the case of certain issues, government commissions are appointed, investigations are conducted, and reports are published and publicized at news conferences, but actual behavior change does not occur (Downs, 1972). The bottom line here is whether or not a policy leads to behavior change, and to solution of the social problem underlying the issue. Seldom have agenda scholars studied what happens as the consequence of an issue being high on the policy agenda, thus leading to new policies, although one would expect that real-world indicators *should* subsequently change.

The behavior change impacts of agenda-setting are indicated by the number of anonymous HIV blood tests following the media coverage of a celebrity with AIDS (Figure 5.1). The number of blood tests in Orange County, California, a suburban area near Los Angeles, jumped immediately each time it was publicly disclosed that a noted celebrity had HIV/AIDS: Rock Hudson in 1985, Paul Gann (well known in California for leading the property-tax revolt) in 1987, Magic Johnson in 1991, and tennis star Arthur Ashe in 1992. The highest peak in the number of blood tests followed Magic Johnson's announcement, which particularly encouraged young people and individuals of color (two populations at especially high risk for HIV infection) to have blood tests (Gellert, Weismuller, Higgins, & Maxwell, 1992). However, these spikes in the number of HIV tests due to celebrities' disclosures did not lead to iden-

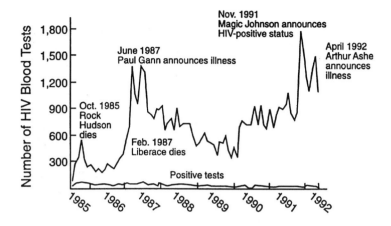

Figure 5.1. News Coverage of the Disclosures by Celebrities That They
Have HIV/AIDS Leads to Increased HIV Testing
SOURCE: Gellert et al. (1992). Reprinted by permission of the *New England Journal of
Medicine,* © 1992, Massachusetts Medical Society.

tification of more individuals with the virus (see the line across the
bottom of Figure 5.1). In other words, the celebrity announcements
mainly motivated the "wrong" people to come forward for HIV blood
tests.

Note one shortcoming of the HIV blood-testing response to media
coverage of celebrities having HIV/AIDS as an indicator of the impacts
of a policy on behavior change. The causal factor being evaluated here
is not really a *new* policy (the federal policy providing HIV blood tests
was implemented much earlier, in the mid-1980s) but the media coverage of celebrities having HIV/AIDS. Thus, the effects of the media
agenda rather than the policy agenda are evidenced by the number of
blood tests. Nevertheless, the current illustration suggests an approach
that could be used to probe overt behavior changes as shown by real-
world indicators due to the implementation of new policies.

We need improved measures of the policy agenda and perhaps a
greater degree of agreement among agenda scholars as to what the most
appropriate measures should be. In comparison, there is a high degree
of consensus that the number of news stories about an issue is a best
measure of the media agenda. And there is a near consensus among hierarchy agenda researchers that poll questions like the MIP are the best

way to measure the public agenda. But scholars who take a single-issue approach (as we detailed in Chapter 4), and policy agenda scholars, index the public agenda and the policy agenda in a variety of ways. The public agenda in single-issue studies may be conceptualized in terms of which special interest groups are able to promote and control the definition of an issue. This is a focus on the active, attentive public, who typically are first exposed to mass media content about issues and then serve as opinion leaders in influencing the views of other members of the public and organizing for action (Weimann, 1994, pp. 281-286). The policy agenda has been indexed by a diversity of variables such as the amount of federal funding appropriated (for coping with an issue), by the creation of a new government agency such as the Environmental Protection Agency in the 1970s, and by the passage of new legislation such as the 1966 auto safety law (Walker, 1977).

Setting the Agenda in the U.S. Senate[3]

Jack L. Walker was a University of Michigan political scientist who investigated the policy agenda-setting process through which the 1966 auto safety law was passed by the U.S. Senate. Previously, Walker had studied the role of various senators and the cliques and coalitions among the senators during their day-to-day political life. Walker then traced the political process through which a crucial auto safety law was passed, thus giving life to the political structure that he had already documented.

Walker focused on the role of legislative champions in proposing new legislation. Most of the Senate's business consists of routine matters that take up most of a senator's time, and so the opportunity to propose a new law is a rare event. In 1962, Abraham Ribicoff was elected to the U.S. Senate after serving as the governor of Connecticut, where he had established a reputation for strongly enforcing highway safety. Ribicoff gained the chairmanship of a Senate subcommittee to investigate the federal government's role in traffic safety. Ralph Nader was a consultant to the subcommittee.

The number of traffic deaths per 100,000 miles driven had declined for 15 years, but in 1960, this real-world indicator turned

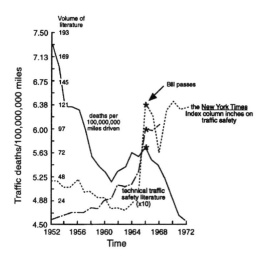

Figure 5.2. The Agenda-Setting Process for the Passage of the Highway Safety Act in 1966
SOURCE: Walker (1977). Used by permission of Cambridge University Press.

sharply upward and rose for the next several years (Figure 5.2). The number of traffic deaths jumped from about 38,000 per year to reach 53,000 in 1966. Research on traffic safety had been under way for a decade, but policymakers had not paid much attention to the findings until various experts were called before the Ribicoff Subcommittee to testify. Some experts argued for more of the same type of programs as in the past: high school driver training courses, for example, and other efforts aimed at the individual driver. This perspective assumed an individual-blame definition of the social problem, that traffic deaths were due to the "nut behind the wheel."

Some technical experts, however, advocated more radical changes, including such automobile redesign as installed seat belts, padded dashboards, and other kinds of crash protection. These system-blame advocates also called for the safer design of highways, such as placing impact attenuators (yellow barrels filled with gravel) in front of viaduct columns. Ralph Nader's 1965 book,

Unsafe at Any Speed, popularized this system-blame viewpoint of auto safety, which argued that unsafe cars and highways were responsible for traffic fatalities, as well as careless drivers.

The *New York Times* news coverage of traffic safety turned upward in 1964 and increased sharply in 1965, the year of the Ribicoff Subcommittee hearings. The *Times*'s coverage then surged in 1966, the peak year in the rate of traffic deaths and the year in which the new law was passed (see Figure 5.1). Walker (1977) concluded from his analysis: "The newspaper was reacting to events, not stimulating the controversy or providing leadership" (p. 435). When the traffic safety legislation reached the stage of formulation and debate, Senator Ribicoff was replaced as the main champion for the new law by Senator Warren Magnuson, the powerful chairman of the Senate Commerce Committee. The passage of the Highway Safety Act was strongly opposed by industrial interests, particularly the U.S. auto industry. But "a majority coalition was discovered in the Senate for an unprecedented expansion of the Federal government's efforts to ensure the safety of its citizens" (Walker, 1977, p. 435). This coalition passed other safety legislation in the years immediately following the 1969 Coal Mine Health and Safety Act as well as the 1970 Occupational Safety and Health Act.

Why did the 1966 traffic safety law pass in the Senate?

An easily understood, widely respected social indicator [traffic deaths] pointed to the development of a serious national problem that prevailing public policies were unable to handle. A body of research with clear policy implications had emerged that provided justification for new legislation. . . . And skillful political entrepreneurs were available who could tie all of these elements together in a dramatic proposal for change. (Walker, 1977, p. 435)

This case illustration demonstrates how policy agenda-setting research can illuminate the exercise of power: "Those who manage to shape the legislative agenda, in other words, are able to magnify their influence many times over by determining the focus of attention and energy in the entire political system" (Walker, 1977, p. 445). Here we see how research on the policy agenda-setting process illuminates the nature of power in the political process.

Summary

This chapter summarized what has been learned about how an issue gets on the policy agenda. Circularity of influence is a consistent finding in policy agenda studies. There is little agreement among agenda-setting scholars on the best way to measure the policy agenda, and indeed, a variety of measures (federal appropriations, a new law, legislative hearings, creation of a new government agency, and so on) have been used.

In some cases, the media agenda has a direct effect in the policy agenda-setting process, although more often, the media agenda has an indirect effect through the public agenda or through prepublication information sharing. The U.S. president is a dominant force on the national policy agenda, but little scholarly research has investigated how the president's agenda is set. *Alternative specification* is the process of narrowing the range of possible positions for any one issue as that issue is being set on a policy agenda. And, as in the case of media agenda-setting and public agenda-setting, an issue is often boosted up the policy agenda by a *trigger event*, defined as a cue-to-action that occurs at a point in time and serves to crystallize attention and action.

Notes

1. This case illustration is based on Martin Linsky (1986) as well as other sources.
2. This case illustration is based on David L. Protess, Fay Lomax Cook, Jack Doppelt, James S. Ettema, Margaret T. Gordon, Donna R. Leff, and Peter Miller (1991), Harvey L. Molotch, D. L. Protess, and M. T. Gordon (1987), and other sources.
3. The following case illustration is based on Jack L. Walker (1977).

6. *Studying the Agenda-Setting Process*

The biggest obstacles that bedevil the transition from [public consciousness to working through social problems] relate to what is sometimes referred to as the "agenda-setting" function of the press.

Daniel Yankelovich (1991, p. 86)

Institutions are often the children of agenda access, and the means through which short periods of attention affect outcomes and government policies for decades.

Frank R. Baumgartner and
Bryan D. Jones (1993, p. 84)

The main theme of this book is a broadening of scholarly research on the agenda-setting process in recent years from hierarchy studies to include investigations of a single issue (or a small interacting number of issues), either studied over time in a sociological approach or studied experimentally in a psychological approach. This paradigmatic change is part of a more general trend toward disaggregation in agenda-setting research. Reasons for this move toward disaggregation are discussed in this chapter.

In this volume, we reviewed the nature of media, public, and policy agenda-setting. Separate chapters were devoted to cross-sectional hierarchy designs versus longitudinal research designs about public agenda-setting. Different methods for studying each of these types of agenda-setting are required. The hierarchy approach to studying public agenda-setting has been dominated by one-point-in-time correlational comparisons of media content with the aggregated responses by the public to survey questions about issue salience. In recent years, however, longitudinal studies have begun to replace the dominance of the multiple-issue hierarchy approach. Investigations of how the media agenda is set now include over-time participant observation in media organizations as well as the analysis of quantitative variables (like real-world indicators). Studies of policy agenda-setting display more variation in method, from depth interviews with elites, to surveys of public leaders, to time-series analyses of congressional voting behavior. Each research method has strengths and weaknesses. Bias of different types is inherent in each method.

This final chapter (a) critiques past research on the agenda-setting process and suggests directions for future work, and (b) identifies ways of combining research methods to increase the validity and reliability of observations and to allow study of new aspects of the entire agenda-setting process.

Comparisons Among Agenda-Setting Approaches

The more than 350 scholarly publications about the agenda-setting process included in our Suggested Readings represent a diversity of research approaches. These varied studies have certain aspects in common. Most are influenced by the agenda-setting metaphor. "One strength of the robust agenda concept is its ability to pull together previously unconnected lines of research" (Reese, 1991, p. 310). Agenda-setting is an exciting idea, and it has attracted a tremendous amount of research attention. It still does. About 25 agenda-setting publications have appeared annually in recent years. The agenda research approach originally promised to illuminate more clearly whether the mass media had effects. "Walter Lippmann's quest in *Public Opinion* to link the world outside to the pictures in our heads via the news media was brought to quantitative, empirical fruition by agenda-setting research" (McCombs, 1992, p. 815).

McCombs and Shaw (1972) justified agenda-setting research as an improved approach to understanding media effects. Have we accomplished what they envisioned several decades ago? The media agenda is powerful in its impact because it usually launches the agenda-setting process. "This media agenda simultaneously projects forward a powerful structuring effect on audience perceptions, while itself indicating the powerful influences behind its creation" (Reese, 1991, p. 309).

Longitudinal studies of agenda-setting are one of relatively few types of over-time investigations in communication research. Longitudinal research allows for the charting of "positive feedback" within a political system, in which small inputs by active, organized groups of issue proponents can cascade into major effects, similar to bandwagon effects, through "issue expansion" (Baumgartner & Jones, 1993). This diffusion of an issue within a system is another way of conceptualizing what

Downs (1972) termed the *issue-attention cycle* as an issue is popularized and institutionalized, or not. Longitudinal perspectives on issue development reveal the exponential growth function characteristic of the diffusion of innovations (Rogers, 1995). As Brosius and Kepplinger (1992a) pointed out:

> Compared to cross-sectional analyses, longitudinal or time-series analyses provide several advantages . . . one can determine the direction of influence of the agenda-setting process (whether media coverage precedes and influences public opinion, or vice versa). Second, one can determine the strength of influence for different issues, and thus define attributes of issues that are contingent conditions for media effects. Third, one can distinguish time periods with either strong or weak media effects, and thus analyze media effects at different points in an issue's history. (pp. 5-6)

It is the longitudinal aspect of certain agenda-setting research designs, both quantitative and qualitative, that allows them to illuminate the nature of media effects with special clarity at a sociological level of analysis, just as it is the control of experimental designs that allows them to illuminate the nature of media effects with special clarity at a psychological level of analysis.

Generalizations About Agenda-Setting

We conclude the previous five chapters with the following generalizations about the agenda-setting process.

1. A common finding of numerous agenda-setting researchers, dating back to the original study by McCombs and Shaw (1972), is that *at a given point, or over a certain period of time, different media place a similar salience on a set of issues*. This similarity of issue saliences in media coverage does not mean that all media are saying exactly the same thing at the same time. Indeed, some studies comparing television with newspaper coverage show that these media differ at times in how they cover an issue. But, in general, *the media tend to agree in the number of, or the proportion of, news stories that they devote to a particular issue*. The media agenda is a very gross indicator of media message content; an agenda-setting investigator does not care what the media say about an issue of study, just *how much* they say about it.

2. *Real-world indicators are relatively unimportant in setting the media agenda.* Funkhouser (1973b), one of the first scholars to compare the media coverage of an issue with a real-world indicator of that issue, found little correspondence. For example, American involvement in Vietnam peaked in 1968, but media coverage had peaked 2 years earlier, in 1966. Real-world indicators for the War on Drugs issue and the environmental issue were continuously improving during the years in which these issues climbed the national agenda (Ader, 1993). In these two cases, the real-world indicator is *negatively* related to the media agenda. Clearly, what counts is the attention that organized networks of people can muster concerning their framing of a problem (Blumer, 1971), and not so much the severity of the problem.

3. *The agenda-setting process is one of social construction through which key individuals interpret clues from the media and from their environment to determine the salience of an issue.* Trigger events (such as the 1984 BBC film clip on the Ethiopian famine) are more important than real-world indicators in putting an issue on the agenda. Agenda-setting is, in some cases, an emotional reaction to certain trigger events.

Unless an issue is perceived as a social problem, at least to a certain degree, it probably will not get on the media agenda. But real-world indicators are usually dry statistics, without much news value and with little impact on the media agenda, unless they are illustrated by a tragic event or a personal tragedy.

4. *The White House, the* New York Times, *and spectacular trigger events play a dominant role in putting an issue on the U.S. media agenda.* Examples of trigger events are the death of Rock Hudson due to AIDS and the Exxon *Valdez* oil spill. Such human drama simplifies a complex issue. Disasters and tragedies help newspersons and the public attach meaning to an event by linking it to an issue.

Can an issue climb the agenda without a trigger event like Rock Hudson or the Exxon *Valdez?* Sometimes. The guns-and-violence issue of 1993-1994 was not tied to any particular personal tragedy or disastrous event. We conclude that *cues-to-action can help an issue climb the national agenda, but these trigger events are not necessary or sufficient.*

5. *Scientific research results do not play an important role in the agenda-setting process.* Looking back across the case illustrations in our previous five chapters, we seldom encountered any role for scientific findings in putting an issue on the media agenda. In the Rogers et al. (1991) study of AIDS in the 1980s, several important scientific breakthroughs (such

as determining that the exchange of bodily fluids was the means of AIDS transmission, identification of the AIDS virus, and finding an HIV blood test) were announced and featured in media news stories. These scientific events, however, did not set the media agenda for the issue of AIDS. Jack Walker's (1977) analysis of the vehicle safety issue in the mid-1960s showed that considerable scientific research had been conducted on ways to lower the rate of traffic deaths through the design of safer vehicles and highways. This research had been widely reported in the scientific literature during the decade prior to passage of the 1966 auto safety law by the U.S. Congress. However, this safety research had no impact on the policy agenda-setting process until its main results were championed by key senators such as Ribicoff and Magnuson.

6. *The position of an issue on the media agenda importantly determines that issue's salience on the public agenda.* Of the 112 empirical studies of the agenda-setting process that we reviewed, 60% support a media agenda-public agenda relationship. Most of these studies were cross-sectional. Subsequent longitudinal investigations continue to support this generalization (Trumbo, 1995). When the media give heavy news coverage to an issue, the public usually responds by according the issue a higher salience on the public agenda. This relationship of the media agenda to the public agenda seems to hold under a wide variety of conditions, for a diversity of issues, and when explored with diverse research methods.

Does the public agenda influence the policy agenda? Here the research evidence is less strong, although the recent large-scale investigation by Erikson et al. (1993) of public opinion and policy positions concludes a strong effect of public opinion on state-level policy making. Other factors also influence the policy agenda (see Figure 4.3).

Toward Disaggregation in Agenda-Setting Research

A powerful paradigm in any scientific specialty can be dangerous in that a single approach to the central research problem may become overly standardized (Kuhn, 1962/1970). Agenda-setting research may have become overly stereotyped around the McCombs and Shaw (1972) paradigm. "The literature on agenda-setting has been stunningly successful in telling people what data to collect but it has not been very successful in telling its readers why the data matter" (Ettema et al., 1991, p. 76). Another critic of the agenda-setting paradigm, Burd (1991), noted: "Unfortunately, too many agenda-setting researchers rely on a linear, one-dimensional, assembly-line model for the production and manufacture of public opinion and policy" (p. 291).

How can such criticisms of the agenda-setting paradigm be overcome? *A long-term trend in agenda-setting research is toward disaggregation of the data.* The original McCombs and Shaw (1972) study was highly aggregated: All of the 100 undecided voters' issue priorities were pooled in one composite ranking of the five main issues of study. The number of news stories in the nine mass media (five newspapers, two newsmagazines, and two television networks' evening news broadcasts) were pooled in one aggregated ranking of the same five issues (foreign policy, law and order, fiscal policy, public welfare, and civil rights). Using less aggregated approaches allows scholars greater insight into the relationships of key variables in the agenda-setting process—relationships that are otherwise masked.

An important move toward data disaggregation is represented by the Erbring et al. (1980) study. These scholars gathered personal interview data from a national sample of respondents in 1974 (to measure the public agenda) and correlated it with the media agenda (of newspaper coverage, which was content-analyzed).

> For those 94 newspapers *actually read* by seven or more of the 1974 survey respondents, all front-page articles (about 8,900) were manually coded for issue content and merged with the survey data by *matching each respondent* with content information from the particular paper he or she had read. (Erbring et al., 1980, pp. 20-21)

As a further step toward localization as a means of disaggregation of the agenda data, *these scholars measured crime and unemployment rates in the communities where their survey respondents lived* (rather than using nationwide real-world indicators for crime and unemployment). They then used these localized real-world indicators in their data analysis. Thus, the media agenda variables, the public agenda variables, and the real-world indicators were disaggregated to the individual and localized level of analysis. This basic change from the much more aggregated approach of the original McCombs and Shaw (1972) study allowed Erbring et al. (1980) to bring the personal characteristics of their respondents into their analysis. They found that issues on the newspaper agenda had greater impact on individuals who were sensitive to a particular issue. For example, elderly and female respondents were more fearful of crime. The media agenda for the crime issue had almost no impact on other audience individuals. This conclusion could not have been investigated through survey research without a high degree of disaggregation.

Other types of localization are also possible as part of a disaggregation strategy. At a given point in time, when the health care issue may top the national agenda, the drunk driving issue tops the agenda in the state of New Mexico, AIDS is the priority in San Francisco, and a particular individual who is out of work in Des Moines perceives that unemployment is the most important problem facing the nation. There may be a relationship of the agenda-setting process at one level with that at another level, but not necessarily.

Further, certain racial or other segments of U.S. society may have an agenda-setting process that operates independently of the national agenda-setting process. For example, Cherry (1986) found that black people in the United States, in answer to national polls, ranked a different set of issues in high priority than did the white population. Black Americans read *Jet, Ebony*, and other distinctive media whose media agenda of issues corresponds closely to the public agenda of issues for African Americans. Perhaps Hispanics have a unique agenda-setting process also, as do other segments of the national population.

Single-issue research or a comparative case study design for the agenda-setting process is one type of disaggregation. Sociological single-issue studies allow scholars to conduct longitudinal time-series analyses of agenda-setting variables, thus allowing insight into the processual aspects of agenda-setting. Experimentation too represents a longitudinal disaggregation strategy, in that one variable, such as the salience of an issue on the media agenda, is manipulated, and the effect of this treatment manipulation on the public agenda of the experimental subjects is tested at the individual level of analysis.

We see similar promise in the nascent use of computer software content analysis programs, such as Wordlink, developed by James Danowski at the University of Illinois at Chicago, and Negopy, a network analysis program developed by Bill Richards at Simon Fraser University in British Columbia. Wordlink was combined with Negopy by Maria Hibbs (1993) in her over-time agenda-setting study of the steel trade issue:

"Words in the text are codes or symbols for the ideas and positions of actors within the issue network. By conducting the word network analysis of the text of news articles and government documents and records, it is possible to explore the word network's structure." (p. 120)

Research Questions for Future Study

Despite more than 350 publications, several vital research questions about the agenda-setting process have not been answered. The following questions might be addressed in future studies of the agenda-setting process.

(1) Who else puts an issue on the national agenda? What institutions in addition to the *New York Times* and the White House put an issue on the national agenda? Does influence between nations in determining which problems come to be recognized as international issues follow a similar logic as we understand for domestic agenda-setting?

(2) What keeps an issue on the national agenda over a lengthy period of time? Can the length of time that an issue is on the agenda be managed? Most issues rise and then fall on the national agenda, usually after being at the top only for a rather short period of several months or years. The War on Drugs issue rose and fell on the national agenda from 1986 to 1991. Yet other issues, AIDS, for example, once on the media agenda (in 1985) stayed there, although with some ups and downs. Is this staying ability of the AIDS issue because of its life-and-death nature, because of the lack of a cure, or for some other reason? How does the context of an issue's rise onto an agenda, whether one of enthusiasm or criticism (Baumgartner & Jones, 1993), affect issue duration? Why does an issue drop down the agenda and disappear? Very few studies have investigated this issue.

(3) What is the nature of the private process of agenda-setting that often may occur prior to the public process that scholars typically observe and report? For instance, in the mid-1980s, such powerful individuals as Frank Stanton, former president of CBS, persuaded Jay Winsten, the Harvard public health professor, to launch the designated driver campaign with Hollywood prime-time television scriptwriters. Thanks to Stanton, Winsten's designated driver issue became relevant among the

top officials in the Hollywood television industry (Montgomery, 1993). Seldom, however, can scholars glimpse such behind-the-scenes aspects of agenda-setting. Such low-profile processes should be illuminated, perhaps through the use of case studies, participant observation, depth interviews, and field methods of inquiry.

(4) What is the role of an issue proponent in the agenda-setting process? Charismatic and persistent issue proponents seem to be necessary for launching certain issues, such as rock musician Bob Geldoff for the 1984 Ethiopian famine and former *San Francisco Chronicle* reporter Randy Shilts for the issue of AIDS in San Francisco. Would these issues have progressed through the agenda-setting process without these issue champions? Political scientists and sociologists, in conducting case studies of political or social actors, have a great deal to teach communication researchers about the role of issue proponents.

(5) Do the proponents responsible for the policy agenda-setting of one issue learn from prior experiences with the agenda-setting process for other issues? Is there any carryover or generalizability of policy agenda-setting from issue to issue? Walker's (1977) study of the 1966 Highway Safety Act suggests that its enactment by the U.S. Senate led directly to later passage of the Mine Safety Act. Thus, one issue may clear the way for a closely related issue. Does this happen often?

(6) How is an issue framed, by whom, and with what regularity? Jay Winsten's designated driver issue focused on drunk driving, but not on alcoholism. The alcoholism issue is threatening to the U.S. television industry, which depends on alcohol advertising sales. AIDS was framed initially as a gay men's disease, then reframed as a minority health problem. Although the framing of an issue is very important, it may happen in a rather accidental way. For example, a spectacular and tragic event may frame an issue. Such framing by a trigger device can then propel the issue through the agenda-setting process. For instance, the Exxon *Valdez* oil spill in March 1989, and how it was framed by the media, helped put the environmental issue on the U.S. policy agenda.

(7) To what degree is the agenda-setting process for an issue in a local community similar to what happens nationally for the same issue? Do issues usually begin locally and then bubble up to the national level? For example, the designated driver campaign began in Boston when a

local TV newscaster was killed by a drunk driver. Two years later, Jay Winsten launched the designated driver issue nationally by influencing Hollywood scriptwriters. Another example is the AIDS issue, which was high on the local agenda in San Francisco for several years before it climbed the national agenda in the United States. The DWI (driving while intoxicated) issue in Albuquerque and in the state of New Mexico in 1993 led to new state laws providing particularly harsh penalties for drunk drivers. It was set off by an event, the 1992 Christmas Eve deaths of three members of a young family who were hit by a drunk driver. Will the DWI issue eventually spread from New Mexico to the national agenda?

(8) What is the end of the agenda-setting process? Why can a short-lived hot glare of mass media attention result in the creation of institutions that then persist for decades, rather independently of social problems? Does a new policy that is adopted as a consequence of the agenda-setting process have an ultimate effect in bringing about social change? Does the new policy solve the social problem that launched the agenda-setting process? Usually, an end goal of an agenda-setting process is individual-level behavior change: smoking cessation, recycling, condom use and safer sex, and designated driving.

One policy effect of the post-1989 environmental crisis was to encourage the public to adopt pro-environmental attitudes toward recycling. Did it affect overt behavior? Derksen and Gartrell (1993) investigated the recycling of cans, bottles, and newspapers in two Canadian cities: Edmonton, which had curbside pickup of recycled materials, and Calgary, which did not have such a program. The generally favorable attitudes toward recycling were highly related to actual recycling behavior in Edmonton, but not in Calgary. Thus, whether or not the high priority of the environmental issue on the public agenda led to actual recycling behavior depended on whether or not a city recycling program was in operation. So, other factors (such as infrastructural variables) intervene in whether the agenda-setting process leads to behavioral change.

(9) Why are some issues not resolved? Homelessness, for example, seems to be an unsolvable problem in the United States. The War on Drugs in the late 1980s was preceded by an earlier drug eradication program in the 1970s. Similarly, the 1990s environmental crisis resulting from the Exxon *Valdez* oil spill is the second time that the environmental issue

has climbed the national agenda in the past 25 years. Some social problems persist despite human attempts to resolve them. These long-term problems are occasionally made anew into "issues" through certain trigger devices and/or issue champions.

(10) How does one issue compete for salience with another issue? In 1990-1991, the Gulf War pushed all other issues off of the U.S. agenda for a period of several months. Do such dominant issues occur very frequently? How do media gatekeepers decide that a certain issue should overshadow another issue? What criteria are used to decide on the amount of news coverage to give to an issue? This dynamic of issue competition has rarely been addressed (Hilgartner & Bosk, 1988). The media agenda and the public agenda can be zero-sum games. How does this issue competition actually occur?

(11) Is the media agenda-setting process limited to news issues? Can entertainment media content affect the public agenda for an issue? The previously cited example of the designated driver campaign in the United States, which boosted awareness of the concept and led to an increase in the use of designated drivers, was mainly accomplished through prime-time television shows, supplemented by public service announcements. The unexplored issue here is whether media content other than news (such as entertainment and advertising) plays a role in the agenda-setting process.

(12) How is the agenda-setting process in other nations different from this process in the United States? Most of the more than 350 agenda-setting publications have a made-in-the-U.S.A. label. Brosius and Kepplinger (1990) and Takeshita (1993), for example, suggest strong similarities between public agenda-setting in Germany and Japan with this process in the United States. Studies have also been carried out in Australia (Gadir, 1982), Canada (Winter, Eyal, & Rogers, 1982), Denmark (Siune & Borre, 1975), Ghana (Anokwa & Salwen, 1988), Saudi Arabia (Al-Haqeel & Melkote, 1994), Singapore (Holaday & Kuo, 1992), Sweden (Asp, 1983), and Venezuela (Chaffee & Izcaray, 1975). Although these studies and those carried out in Germany and Japan provide valuable information about comparative media functions in less industrially developed and more industrially developed nations, more research in a wider variety of countries is needed.

The Need for Multimethod Research Designs

Brewer and Hunter (1989), Yin (1989), and Shadish, Cook, and Leviton (1991) argue for the strategic combination of different research methods that vary in their types of inherent bias. *Multimethod research* is a systematic inquiry that combines several different data-gathering methods. A *complementary multimethod approach* is a research design in which each method provides data about different but related research questions. A *focused multimethod approach* is a research design in which each method provides different data in a strong test of the same hypothesis or research question.

There are also disadvantages of conducting multimethod research. Using different methods of data gathering requires more preparation and planning in the design of a research project. More resources (time, money, and collaborators or assistants) are usually required. A wider range of competencies is required of multimethod investigators. They must understand each of the methods they use. Despite these difficulties, multimethod research on the agenda-setting process is needed. In the past, most investigations have measured each variable with a single data-gathering method.

Agenda-Setting in Democratic Societies

What is the unique contribution of the agenda-setting perspective? It "implicitly adopts the pluralistic values of democratic theory, bringing public opinion to center stage" (Reese, 1991, p. 310). This emphasis on public opinion is especially characteristic of conceptualizations of the entire agenda-setting process where public opinion plays a deterministic role.

What assumptions about the media, public opinion, and democracy do agenda-setting scholars make? "No doubt most agenda researchers . . . are motivated by the notion that they have isolated a key moment in the process of governance" (Ettema et al., 1991, p. 76). Ideally, in American democratic theory, "the press monitors the political environment, contributes to the formation of public opinion, and, thereby, motivates policy initiatives." So, one crucial assumption about the agenda-setting process is that the media agenda often launches the process, putting an issue on the public agenda, which then may lead to policy change. This instigating role for the mass media highlights a crucial role they play in a democratic society.

* * *

On the twentieth anniversary of agenda-setting research, McCombs and Shaw (1993) concluded that recent studies suggest more than a limited effect on cognition. Under certain conditions, the media of mass communication tell us how to think about issues and, therefore, what to think. We agree. The public agenda-setting effects of media are more powerful than indicated by Bernard Cohen (1963), with whose quotation we began this book. Fascinating studies that explore the political nature of policy agenda-setting, the diverse sources of influence on media agendas, and the use of multiple methods to study the longitudinal dynamics of media, public, and policy agenda-setting are being published. Taken together, such research offers to raise the sights of students of agenda-setting from the testing of a hypothesis to holistic investigations of social influence.

References[1]

Ader, C. R. (1993, August). *A longitudinal study of agenda-setting for the issue of environmental pollution*. Paper presented at the Association for Education in Journalism and Mass Communication, Kansas City.

Al-Haqeel, A. S., & Melkote, S. R. (1994). *International agenda-setting effects of Saudi Arabian media: A case study*. Paper presented at the Association for Education in Journalism and Mass Communication, Atlanta.

Anokwa, K., & Salwen, M. B. (1988). Newspaper agenda-setting among elites and non-elites in Ghana. *Gazette, 41,* 201-214.

Ansolabehere, S., & Iyengar, S. (1994). Riding the wave and claiming ownership over issues: The joint effects of advertising and news coverage in campaigns. *Public Opinion Quarterly, 58,* 335-357.

Asp, K. (1983). The struggle for agenda: Party agenda, media agenda and voter agenda in the 1979 Swedish election campaign. *Communication Research, 10*(3), 333-355.

Ball-Rokeach, S. (1985). The origins of individual media system dependency: Sociological framework. *Communication Research, 12,* 485-510.

Baumgartner, F. R., & Jones, B. D. (1993). *Agendas and instability in American politics.* Chicago: University of Chicago Press.

Blumer, H. (1948). Public opinion and public opinion polling. *American Sociological Review, 13*(5), 542-554.

Blumer, H. (1971). Social problems as collective behavior. *Social Problems, 18*(3), 298-306.

Boorstin, D. (1961). *The image.* New York: Harper.

Boot, W. (1985, March-April). Ethiopia: Feasting on famine. *Columbia Journalism Review,* pp. 47-48.

Bosso, C. J. (1987). *Pesticides and politics: The life cycle of a public issue.* Pittsburgh: University of Pittsburgh Press.

Brecher, M., Steinberg, B., & Stein, J. (1969). A framework for research on foreign policy behavior. *Journal of Conflict Resolution, 13*(1), 75-101.

Brewer, J., & Hunter, A. (1989). *Multimethod research.* Newbury Park, CA: Sage.

Brosius, H., & Kepplinger, H. M. (1990). The agenda-setting function of television news: Static and dynamic views. *Communication Research, 17*(2), 183-211.

Brosius, H., & Kepplinger, H. M. (1992a). Linear and non linear models of agenda setting in television. *Journal of Broadcasting and Electronic Media, 36,* 5-32.

Brosius, H., & Kepplinger, H. M. (1992b, May). *In search of killer issues: Issue competition in the agenda-setting process*. Paper presented at the American Association for Public Opinion Research, St. Petersburg, FL.

---

1. A comprehensive bibliography of agenda-setting publications begins on page 109.

Burd, G. (1991). A critique of two decades of agenda-setting research. In D. E. Protess & M. McCombs (Eds.), *Agenda-setting: Readings on media, public opinion, and policymaking* (pp. 291-294). Hillsdale, NJ: Lawrence Erlbaum.

Carragee, K., Rosenblatt, M., & Michaud, G. (1987). Agenda-setting research: A critique and theoretical alternative. In S. Thomas (Ed.), *Studies in communication 3* (pp. 35-49). Norwood, NJ: Ablex.

Chaffee, S. H., & Izcaray, F. (1975). Mass communication functions in a media rich developing society. In S. H. Chaffee (Ed.), *Political communication: Issues and strategies for research* (pp. 367-395). Beverly Hills, CA: Sage.

Cherry, D. (1986). *A longitudinal analysis of the agenda-setting power of the black periodical press.* Unpublished doctoral dissertation, University of North Carolina, Chapel Hill.

Cobb, R. W., & Elder, C. D. (1981). Communication and public policy. In D. D. Nimmo & K. R. Sanders (Eds.), *Handbook of political communication* (pp. 391-416). Beverly Hills, CA: Sage.

Cobb, R. W., & Elder, C. D. (1983). *Participation in American politics: The dynamics of agenda-building.* Baltimore: Johns Hopkins University Press. (Original work published by Allyn & Bacon in 1972)

Cohen, B. C. (1963). *The press and foreign policy.* Princeton, NJ: Princeton University Press.

Cohen, B. C. (1965). *Foreign policy in American government.* Boston: Little, Brown.

Cohen, M., March, J., & Olsen, J. (1972). A garbage can model of organizational choice. *Administrative Science Quarterly, 17,* 1-25.

Crane, D. (1972). *Invisible colleges: Diffusion of knowledge in scientific communities.* Chicago: University of Chicago Press.

Danielian, L., & Reese, S. (1989). A closer look at intermedia influences on agenda-setting: The cocaine issue of 1986. In P. J. Shoemaker (Ed.), *Communication campaigns about drugs: Government, media and the public* (pp. 47-64). Hillsdale, NJ: Lawrence Erlbaum.

Davis, F. J. (1952). Crime news in Colorado newspapers. *American Journal of Sociology, 57,* 325-330.

Dearing, J. W. (1989). Setting the polling agenda for the issue of AIDS. *Public Opinion Quarterly, 53*(3), 309-329.

Dearing, J. W. (1992). Foreign blood and domestic politics: The issue of AIDS in Japan. In E. Fee & D. M. Fox (Eds.), *AIDS: The making of a chronic disease* (pp. 326-345). Berkeley: University of California Press.

Dearing, J. W., & Rogers, E. M. (1992). AIDS and the media agenda. In T. Edgar, M. Fitzpatrick, & V. Freimuth (Eds.), *AIDS: A communication perspective* (pp. 173-194). Hillsdale, NJ: Lawrence Erlbaum.

DeFleur, M. L. (1987). The growth and decline of research on the diffusion of the news 1945-1985. *Communication Research, 14*(1), 109-130.

Derksen, L., & Gartrell, J. (1993). The social context of recycling. *American Sociological Review, 58,* 434-442.

Deutschmann, P. J., & Danielson, W. (1960). Diffusion of the major news story. *Journalism Quarterly, 37,* 345-355.

Downs, A. (1972). Up and down with ecology: The issue-attention cycle. *Public Interest, 28,* 38-50.

Eichhorn, W. (1993, August). *An experimental test of the agenda-setting function of the press.* Paper presented at the Association for Education in Journalism and Mass Communication, Kansas City.

Einsiedel, E. F., Salomone, K. L., & Schneider, F. P. (1984). Crime: Effects of media exposure and personal experience on issue salience. *Journalism Quarterly, 61,* 131-136.

103

Entman, R. M. (1989). How the media affect what people think: An information processing approach. *Journal of Politics, 51,* 347-370.

Erbring, L., Goldenberg, E. N., & Miller, A. H. (1980). Front-page news and real-world cues: A new look at agenda-setting by the media. *American Journal of Political Science, 24*(1), 16-49.

Erikson, R. S., Wright, G. C., & McIver, J. P. (1993). *Statehouse democracy: Public opinion and policy in the American states.* New York: Cambridge University Press.

Ettema, J. S., Protess, D. L., Leff, D. R., Miller, P. V., Doppelt, J., & Cook, F. L. (1991). Agenda-setting as politics: A case study of the press-public-policy connection. *Communication, 12,* 75-98.

Eyal, C. H. (1979). *Time-frame in agenda setting research: A study of the conceptual and methodological factors affecting the time frame context of the agenda-setting process.* Unpublished doctoral dissertation, Syracuse University, Syracuse, NY.

Eyal, C., Winter, J. P., & DeGeorge, W. F. (1981). The concept of time frame in agenda-setting. In G. C. Wilhoit & H. DeBock (Eds.), *Mass communication review yearbook 2* (pp. 212-218). Beverly Hills, CA: Sage.

Fiske, S., & Taylor, S. (1984). *Social cognition.* New York: Random House.

Fitzgerald, F. (1986). *Cities on a hill: A journey through contemporary American culture.* New York: Simon & Schuster.

Funkhouser, G. R. (1973a). The issues of the sixties: An exploratory study in the dynamics of public opinion. *Public Opinion Quarterly, 37*(1), 62-75.

Funkhouser, G. R. (1973b). Trends in media coverage of the issues of the sixties. *Journalism Quarterly, 50,* 533-538.

Gadir, S. (1982). Media agenda-setting in Australia: The rise and fall of public issues. *Media Information Australia, 26,* 13-23.

Gamson, W. A. (1975). *The strategy of protest.* Homewood, IL: Dorsey.

Gamson, W. A. (1992). *Talking politics.* Cambridge: Cambridge University Press.

Gans, H. J. (1979). *Deciding what's news: A study of CBS Evening News, NBC Nightly News, Newsweek and Time.* New York: Pantheon.

Gellert, G. A., Weismuller, P. C., Higgins, K. V., & Maxwell, R. M. (1992). Disclosure of AIDS in celebrities. *New England Journal of Medicine, 327*(19), 1389.

Goodman, R. (1994, May). *Bush administration congressional versus presidential agenda-setting: The China most favored nation controversy.* Paper presented at the International Communication Association, Albuquerque.

Heclo, H. (1978). Issue networks and the executive establishment. In A. King (Ed.), *The new American political system* (pp. 87-124). Washington, DC: American Enterprise Institute.

Hertog, J. K., Finnegan, J. R., Jr., & Kahn, E. (1994). Media coverage of AIDS, cancer, and sexually transmitted diseases: A test of the public arenas model. *Journalism Quarterly, 71*(2), 291-304.

Hibbs, M. P. (1993). *A crossfire of information: A network approach to the agenda-setting hypothesis of the press: The case of steel trade.* Unpublished doctoral dissertation, University of Illinois, Chicago.

Hilgartner, S., & Bosk, C. L. (1988). The rise and fall of social problems: A public arenas model. *American Journal of Sociology, 94*(1), 53-78.

Holaday, D., & Kuo, E. (1992, August). *Upsetting the agenda: Media and the 1991 Singapore election.* Paper presented at the Association for Education in Journalism and Mass Communication, Montreal.

Iyengar, S. (1991). *Is anyone responsible? How television frames political issues.* Chicago: University of Chicago Press.

104

Iyengar, S., & Kinder, D. R. (1985). Psychological accounts of media agenda-setting. In S. Kraus & R. M. Perloff (Eds.), *Mass media and political thought* (pp. 117-140). Beverly Hills, CA: Sage.

Iyengar, S., & Kinder, D. R. (1987). *News that matters: Television and American opinion.* Chicago: University of Chicago Press.

Iyengar, S., Peters, M. D., & Kinder, D. R. (1982). Experimental demonstrations of the 'not-so-minimal' consequences of television news programs. *American Political Science Review, 76*(4), 848-858.

Jamieson, K. H. (1992). *Dirty politics.* New York: Oxford University Press.

Kerr, P. (1986, November 17). Anatomy of an issue: Drugs, the evidence, the reaction. *New York Times,* pp. 1, 12.

Kingdon, J. W. (1984). *Agendas, alternatives, and public policies.* Boston: Little, Brown.

Kuhn, T. S. (1970). *The structure of scientific revolutions.* Chicago: University of Chicago Press. (Original work published 1962)

Lang, G. E., & Lang, K. (1981). Watergate: An exploration of the agenda-building process. In G. C. Wilhoit & H. DeBock (Eds.), *Mass communication review yearbook 2* (pp. 447-468). Beverly Hills, CA: Sage.

Lasswell, H. D. (1927). *Propaganda technique in the world war.* New York: Knopf.

Lasswell, H. D. (1948). The structure and function of communication in society. In L. Bryson (Ed.), *The communication of ideas: A series of addresses.* New York: Harper.

Lazarsfeld, P. F., & Merton, R. K. (1964). Mass communication, popular taste and organized social action. In L. Bryson (Ed.), *The communication of ideas: A series of addresses* (pp. 95-118). New York: Harper. (Original work published 1948)

Liebes, T., & Katz, E. (1990). *The export of meaning.* New York: Oxford University Press.

Linsky, M. (1986). *How the press affects federal policy making.* New York: Norton.

Linsky, M., Moore, J., O'Donnell, W., & Whitman, D. (1986). *How the press affects federal policy-making: Six cases studies.* New York: Norton.

Lippmann, W. (1922). *Public opinion.* New York: Harcourt Brace.

Lipsky, M. (1968). Protest as a political resource. *American Political Science Review, 62,* 1144-1158.

Lowi, T. J. (1964). American business, public policy, case studies and political theory. *World Politics, 16*(4), 677-715.

MacKuen, M. B. (1981). Social communication and the mass policy agenda. In M. B. MacKuen & S. L. Coombs (Eds.), *More than news: Media power in public affairs* (pp. 19-144). Beverly Hills, CA: Sage.

Manheim, J. B. (1986). A model of agenda dynamics. In M. L. McLaughlin (Ed.), *Communication yearbook 10* (pp. 499-516). Newbury Park, CA: Sage.

Mansbach, R. W., & Vasquez, J. A. (1981). *In search of theory: A new paradigm for global politics.* New York: Columbia University Press.

Mazur, A. (1981). Media coverage and public opinion on scientific controversies. *Journal of Communication, 31,* 106-115.

Mazur, A. (1987). Putting radon on the public's risk agenda. *Science, Technology and Human Values, 12*(3-4), 86-93.

McCarthy, J. D., & Zald, M. N. (1977). Resource mobilization and social movements: A partial theory. *American Journal of Sociology, 82*(6), 1212-1241.

McCombs, M. E. (1977). Newspaper vs. television: Mass communication effects across time. In D. L. Shaw & M. E. McCombs (Eds.), *The emergence of American political issues: The agenda-setting function of the press* (pp. 89-105). St. Paul, MN: West.

McCombs, M. E. (1981a). The agenda-setting approach. In D. D. Nimmo & K. R. Sanders (Eds.), *Handbook of political communication* (pp. 121-140). Beverly Hills, CA: Sage.

McCombs, M. E. (1981b). Setting the agenda for agenda-setting research: An assessment of the priority, ideas and problems. In G. C. Wilhoit & H. de Beck (Eds.), *Mass communication review yearbook 2* (pp. 219-224). Beverly Hills, CA: Sage.

McCombs, M. E. (1992). Explorers and surveyors: Expanding strategies for agenda-setting research. *Journalism Quarterly, 69*(4), 813-824.

McCombs, M. E., & Shaw, D. L. (1972). The agenda-setting function of the mass media. *Public Opinion Quarterly, 36,* 176-187.

McCombs, M. E., & Shaw, D. L. (1993). The evolution of agenda-setting research: Twenty-five years in the marketplace. *Journal of Communication, 43*(2), 58-67.

McCombs, M., & Zhu, J. (1995). Capacity, diversity, and volatility of the public agenda: Trends from 1954 to 1994. *Public Opinion Quarterly, 59*(4), 495-535.

McLeod, J. M., Becker, L. B., & Byrnes, J. E. (1974). Another look at the agenda-setting function of the press. *Communication Research, 1,* 131-166.

Mead, T. D. (1994). The daily newspaper as political agenda setter: *The Charlotte Observer* and metropolitan reform. *State and Local Government Review, 26*(1), 27-37.

Molotch, H. L., Protess, D. L., & Gordon, M. T. (1987). The media-policy connection: Ecology of news. In D. Paletz (Ed.), *Political communication: Theories, cases and assessments* (pp. 26-42). Norwood, NJ: Ablex.

Montgomery, K. C. (1989). *Target: Prime time—Advocacy groups and the struggle over entertainment television.* New York: Oxford University Press.

Montgomery, K. C. (1993). The Harvard Alcohol Project: Promoting the designated driver on television. In T. E. Backer & E. M. Rogers (Eds.), *Organizational aspects of health communication campaigns: What works?* (pp. 178-202). Newbury Park, CA: Sage.

Morgenthau, H. J. (1948). *Politics among nations: The struggle for power and peace.* New York: Knopf.

Mullins, L. E. (1977). Agenda-setting and the young voter. In D. L. Shaw & M. E. McCombs (Eds.), *The emergence of American political issues: The agenda-setting function of the press* (pp. 133-148). St. Paul, MN: West.

Nader, R. (1965). *Unsafe at any speed.* New York: Grossman.

Nelson, B. J. (1984). *Making an issue of child abuse: Political agenda setting for social problems.* Chicago: University of Chicago Press.

Neuman, W. R. (1990). The threshold of public attention. *Public Opinion Quarterly, 54,* 159-176.

Neuman, W. R., Just, M. R., & Crigler, A. N. (1992). *Common knowledge: News and the construction of political meaning.* Chicago: University of Chicago Press.

Noelle-Neumann, E. (1984). *The spiral of silence.* Chicago: University of Chicago Press.

O'Gorman, H. (1973). Pluralistic ignorance and white estimates of white support for racial segregation. *Public Opinion Quarterly, 39*(3), 313-330.

Palmgreen, P., & Clarke, P. (1977). Agenda-setting with local and national issues. *Communication Research, 4,* 435-452. Park, R. E. (1922). *The immigrant press and its control.* New York: Harper.

Patterson, T. E. (1993). *Out of order.* New York: Knopf.

Ploughman, P. (1984). *The creation of newsworthy events: An analysis of newspaper coverage of the man-made disaster at Love Canal.* Unpublished doctoral dissertation, State University of New York, Buffalo.

106

Price, D., de Sola. (1961). *Science since Babylon*. New Haven, CT: Yale University Press.

Protess, D. L., Cook, F. L., Doppelt, J. C., Ettema, J. S., Gordon, M. T., Leff, D. R., & Miller, P. (1991). *The journalism of outrage*. New York: Guilford.

Protess, D. L., Leff, D. R., Brooks, S. C., & Gordon, M. T. (1985). Uncovering rape: The watchdog press and the limits of agenda-setting. *Public Opinion Quarterly, 49*(1), 19-37.

Reese, S. D. (1991). Setting the media's agenda: A power balance perspective. In J. A. Anderson (Ed.), *Communication yearbook 14* (pp. 309-340). Newbury Park, CA: Sage.

Reinarman, C. (1988). The social construction of an alcohol problem: The case of Mothers Against Drunk Drivers and social control in the 1980's. *Theory and Society, 17*, 91-120.

Rogers, E. M. (1983). *Diffusion of innovations* (3rd ed.). New York: Free Press.

Rogers, E. M. (1994). *A history of communication study: A biographical approach*. New York: Free Press.

Rogers, E. M. (1995). *Diffusion of innovations* (4th ed.). New York: Free Press.

Rogers, E. M., & Chang, S. (1991). Media coverage of technology issues: Ethiopian drought of 1984, AIDS, Challenger and Chernobyl. In L. Wilkens & P. Patterson (Eds.), *Risky business: Communicating issues of science, risk and public policy* (pp. 75-96). New York: Greenwood.

Rogers, E. M., & Dearing, J. W. (1988). Agenda-setting research: Where has it been? Where is it going? In J. A. Anderson (Ed.), *Communication yearbook 11* (pp. 555-594). Newbury Park, CA: Sage.

Rogers, E. M., Dearing, J. W., & Bregman, D. (1993). The anatomy of agenda-setting research. *Journal of Communication, 43*(2A), 68-84.

Rogers, E. M., Dearing, J. W., & Chang, S. (1991). AIDS in the 1980s: The agenda-setting process for a public issue. *Journalism Monographs, 126.*

Rosenau, J. N. (1961). *Public opinion and foreign policy*. New York: Random House.

Rosenau, J. N. (1971). Pre-theories and theories of foreign policy. In J. N. Rosenau (Ed.), *The scientific study of foreign policy*. New York: Free Press.

Salwen, M. B., & Matera, F. R. (1992). Public salience of foreign nations. *Journalism Quarterly, 69*, 623-632.

Schattschneider, E. E. (1960). *The semisovereign people: A realist's view of democracy in America*. New York: Holt, Rinehart & Winston.

Schoenbach, K., & Semetko, H. A. (1992). Agenda-setting, agenda-reinforcing or agenda-deflating? A study of the 1990 German national election. *Journalism Quarterly, 69*(4), 837-846.

Schweitzer, J. C., & Smith, B. L. (1991, Summer). Community pressures on agenda-setting. *Newspaper Research Journal*, pp. 46-62.

Shadish, W. R., Jr., Cook, T. D., & Leviton, L. C. (1991). *Foundations of program evaluation: Theories of practice*. Newbury Park, CA: Sage.

Shaw, D. L., & Clemmer, C. L. (1977). News and the public response. In D. L. Shaw & M. E. McCombs (Eds.), *The emergence of American political issues: The agenda-setting function of the press* (pp. 33-51). St. Paul, MN: West.

Shaw, D. L., & McCombs, M. (1977). *The emergence of American political issues: The agenda-setting function of the press*. St. Paul, MN: West.

Shefner, C. L., & Rogers, E. M. (1992, May). Hollywood lobbyists: How social causes get in network television. Paper presented at the International Communication Association, Miami.

Shoemaker, P. (1991). *Gatekeepers*. Newbury Park, CA: Sage.

Shoemaker, P. J., Wanta, W., & Leggett, D. (1989). Drug coverage and public opinion, 1972-1986. In P. J. Shoemaker (Ed.), *Communication campaigns about drugs: Government, media and the public* (pp. 67-80). Hillsdale, NJ: Lawrence Erlbaum.

Siune, K., & Borre, O. (1975). Setting the agenda for a Danish election. *Journal of Communication, 25*(1), 65-73.

Smith, C. (1993). News sources and power elites in news coverage of the Exxon Valdez spill. *Journalism Quarterly, 70*(2), 393-403.

Smith, T. W. (1980). America's most important problem: A trend analysis, 1946-1976. *Public Opinion Quarterly, 44,* 164-180.

Stone, G. C., & McCombs, M. E. (1981). Tracing the time lag in agenda-setting. *Journalism Quarterly, 58*(1), 51-55.

Takeshita, T. (1993). Agenda-setting effects of the press in a Japanese local election. *Studies of Broadcasting, 29,* 194-216 (NHK).

Tipton, L., Haney, R. D., & Baseheart, J. R. (1975). Media agenda-setting in city and state election campaigns. *Journalism Quarterly, 52*(1), 15-22.

Trumbo, C. (1995). Longitudinal modeling of public issues: An application of the agenda-setting process to the issue of global warming. *Journalism Monographs, 152.*

Walker, J. L. (1977). Setting the agenda in the U.S. Senate: A theory of problem selection. *British Journal of Political Science, 7,* 433-445.

Wallack, L. (1990). Two approaches to health promotion in the mass media. *World Health Forum, 11,* 143-164.

Wanta, W., & Hu, Y. (1994). The effects of credibility, reliance, and exposure on media agenda-setting: A path analysis model. *Journalism Quarterly, 71*(1), 99-109.

Wanta, W., & Wu, Y. (1992). Interpersonal communication and the agenda-setting process. *Journalism Quarterly, 69*(4), 847-855.

Weaver, D. H. (1977). Political issues and voter need for orientation. In D. L. Shaw & M. E. McCombs (Eds.), *The emergence of American political issues: The agenda-setting function of the press* (pp. 107-119). St. Paul, MN: West.

Weaver, D. H. (1984). Media agenda-setting and public opinion: Is there a link? In R. N. Bostrom (Ed.), *Communication yearbook 8* (pp. 680-691). Beverly Hills, CA: Sage.

Weaver, D. H., Graber, D. A., McCombs, M. E., & Eyal, C. H. (1981). *Media agenda-setting in a presidential election: Issues, images and interest* (T. Takeshita, Trans.). New York: Praeger; in Japanese, Tokyo: Keiso-Shabo.

Weaver, D. H., McCombs, M. E., & Spellman, C. (1975). Watergate and the media: A case study of agenda-setting. *American Politics Quarterly, 3,* 458-472.

Weimann, G. (1994). The influentials as leaders and agenda-setters. In G. Weimann, *The influentials: People who influence people.* Albany: State University of New York Press.

Weisman, A. P. (1986, October). I was a drug-hype junkie. *New Republic,* pp. 14-17.

Williams, E. (1993). Personal interview, May 5, as quoted in Timothy D. Mead (1994), The daily newspaper as political agenda setter: The Charlotte Observer and metropolitan reform. *State and Local Government Review, 26*(1), 27-37.

Winter, J. P. (1981). Contingent conditions in the agenda-setting process. *Mass communication review yearbook 2* (pp. 235-243). Beverly Hills, CA: Sage.

Winter, J. P., & Eyal, C. (1981). Agenda-setting for the civil rights issue. *Public Opinion Quarterly, 45,* 376-383.

Winter, J. P., Eyal, C., & Rogers, A. H. (1982). Issue-specific agenda-setting: The whole as less than the number of parts. *Canadian Journal of Communication, 8,* 1-10.

Yankelovich, D. (1991). *Coming to public judgment: Making democracy work in a complex world.* Syracuse, NY: Syracuse University Press.

Yin, R. K. (1989). *Case study research.* Newbury Park, CA: Sage.

Zhu, J. (1992a). Issue competition and attention distraction in agenda-setting: A zero-sum perspective. *Journalism Quarterly, 69*(4), 825-836.

Zhu, J. (1992b). *Media agenda-setting and priming during the deficit crisis and the Gulf War: A time-series analysis.* Unpublished paper, University of Connecticut, Storrs, Department of Communication Science.

Zhu, J., Watt, J. H., Snyder, L. B., Yan, J., & Jiang, Y. (1993). Public issue priority formation: Media agenda-setting and social interaction. *Journal of Communication, 43*(1), 8-29.

Zimmerman, W. (1973). Issue area and foreign-policy process: A research note in search of a general theory. *American Political Science Review, 67*(2), 1204-1212.

Zucker, H. G. (1978). The variable nature of news media influence. In B. D. Ruben (Ed.), *Communication yearbook 2* (pp. 235-246). New Brunswick, NJ: Transaction.

Suggested Readings
About Agenda-Setting[1]

Adams, W. C. (1986). Whose lives count? TV coverage of natural disasters. *Journal of Communication, 36*, 113-122.

Ader, C. R. (1993, August). *A longitudinal study of agenda-setting for the issue of environmental pollution.* Paper presented at the Association for Education in Journalism and Mass Communication, Kansas City.

Al-Haqeel, A. S., & Melkote, S. R. (1994). *International agenda-setting effects of Saudi Arabian media: A case study.* Paper presented at the Association for Education in Journalism and Mass Communication, Atlanta.

Almond, G. A. (1950). *The American people and foreign policy.* New York: Harcourt Brace.

Anokwa, K., & Salwen, M. B. (1986). Newspaper agenda-setting among elites and non-elites in Ghana. *Gazette, 41*, 201-214.

Asp, K. (1983). The struggle for agenda: Party agenda, media agenda and voter agenda in the 1979 Swedish election campaign. *Communication Research, 10*(3), 333-355.

Atwater, T. (1987). *Network evening news coverage of the TWA hostage crisis.* Paper presented at the International Communication Association, Montreal.

Atwater, T., Fico, F., & Pizart, G. (1987). Reporting on the state legislature: A case study of inter-media agenda-setting. *Newspaper Research Journal, 8*(2), 53-62.

Atwater, T., Salwen, M. B., & Anderson, R. B. (1985a). Media agenda-setting with environmental issues. *Journalism Quarterly, 62*(2), 393-397.

Atwater, T., Salwen, M. B., & Anderson, R. B. (1985b). Interpersonal discussion as a potential barrier to agenda-setting. *Newspaper Research Journal, 6*(4), 37-43.

Atwood, L. E. (1978). Daily newspaper contributions to community discussion. *Journalism Quarterly, 55*(7), 570-576.

Atwood, L. E. (1981). From press release to voting reasons: Tracing the agenda in a congressional campaign. In D. Nimmo (Ed.), *Communication yearbook 2* (pp. 467-482). New Brunswick, NJ: Transaction.

---

1. This bibliography includes a wide range of academic publications and papers. Most of the entries explicitly concern the study of media agendas, public agendas, and/or policy agendas. Many entries, however, either were written prior to 1972, when the term *agenda-setting* was first used, or their authors chose to use other terms to describe their scholarly interests. We include those publications and papers here based on our reading of them and our determination that they make a contribution to understanding the broader process of agenda-setting.

Au, N. (1993). *Issue robustness: A content analysis of news articles on AIDS from The New York Times, 1987-1992.* Master's thesis, University of Texas, Austin.

Auh, T. S. (1977). *Issue conflict and mass media agenda-setting.* Unpublished doctoral dissertation, Indiana University: Bloomington.

Bader, R. G. (1990). How science news sections influence newspaper science coverage: A case study. *Journalism Quarterly, 67*(1), 88-96.

Barkin, S. M., & Gurevitch, M. (1987). Out of work and on the air: Television news of unemployment. *Critical Studies in Mass Communication, 4*(1), 1-20.

Basil, M. D., & Brown, W. J. (1994). Interpersonal communication in news diffusion: A study of 'Magic' Johnson's announcement. *Journalism Quarterly, 72*(2), 305-320.

Baumgartner, F. R., & Jones, B. D. (1993). *Agendas and instability in American politics.* Chicago: University of Chicago Press.

Becker, L. B. (1977). The impact of issue salience. In D. L. Shaw & M. E. McCombs (Eds.), *The emergence of American public issues: The agenda-setting function of the press* (pp. 121-131). St. Paul, MN: West.

Becker, L. B. (1982). The mass media and citizen assessment of issue importance: A reflection on agenda-setting research. In D. C. Whitney, E. Wartella, & S. Windahl (Eds.), *Mass communication review yearbook 3* (pp. 521-536). Beverly Hills, CA: Sage.

Becker, L. B. (1991). Reflecting on metaphors. In J. A. Anderson (Ed.), *Communication yearbook 14* (pp. 341-346). Newbury Park, CA: Sage.

Becker, L. B., & McCombs, M. (1978). The role of the press in determining voter reactions to presidential primaries. *Human Communication Research, 4*(4), 301-307.

Becker, L. B., McCombs, M. E., & McLeod, J. M. (1975). The development of political cognitions. In S. H. Chaffee (Ed.), *Political communication: Issues and strategies for research* (pp. 21-63). Beverly Hills, CA: Sage.

Becker, L. B., & McLeod, J. M. (1976). Political consequences of agenda-setting. *Mass Communication Research, 3*, 8-15.

Becker, L. B., Weaver, D. H., Graber, D. H., & McCombs, M. E. (1979). Influence on public agendas. In S. Kraus (Ed.), *The great debates: Carter vs. Ford 1976* (pp. 418-428). Bloomington: Indiana University Press.

Behr, R. L., & Iyengar, S. (1985). Television news, real-world cues, and changes in the public agenda. *Public Opinion Quarterly, 49*(1), 38-57.

Beniger, J. R. (1978). Media content as social indicators: The Greenfield Index of Agenda-Setting. *Communication Research, 5*, 437-453.

Beniger, J. R. (1983). *Trafficking in drug users: Professional exchange networks in the control of deviance.* New York: Cambridge University Press.

Beniger, J. R. (1984). Mass media, contraceptive behavior, and abortion: Toward a comprehensive model of subjective social changes. In C. F. Turner & E. Martin (Eds.), *Surveying subjective phenomena 2* (pp. 475-500). New York: Russell Sage.

Beniger, J. R. (1988). Winning the presidential nomination: National polls and state primary elections, 1936-1972. *Public Opinion Quarterly, 40*(1), 22-38.

Bennett, W. L., & Paletz, D. L. (Eds.). (1994). *Taken by storm: The media, public opinion, and U.S. foreign policy in the Gulf War.* Chicago: University of Chicago Press.

Benton, M., & Frazier, P. J. (1976). The agenda-setting function of the mass media at three levels of information holding. *Communication Research, 3*(2), 261-274.

Berkovitz, D. (1987). TV news sources and news channels: A study in agenda-building. *Journalism Quarterly, 64*(2-3), 508-513.

Berry, N. O. (1990). *Foreign policy and the press: An analysis of the New York Times' coverage of U.S. foreign policy.* New York: Greenwood.

Black, E. R., & Snow, P. (1982). The political agendas of three newspapers and city governments. *Canadian Journal of Communication, 8,* 11-25.

Bloj, A. G. (1975). Into the wild blue yonder: Behavioral implications of agenda-setting for air travel. In *Studies in agenda-setting.* Syracuse, NY: Syracuse University, Newhouse Communications Research Center.

Blood, W. (1982). Agenda-setting: A review of the theory. *Media Information Australia, 26,* 3-12.

Blumer, H. (1971). Social problems as collective behavior. *Social Problems, 18*(3), 298-306.

Bosso, C. J. (1987). *Pesticides and politics: The life cycle of a public issue.* Pittsburgh: University of Pittsburgh Press.

Bowers, T. A. (1973). Newspaper political advertising and the agenda-setting function. *Journalism Quarterly, 50,* 552-556.

Bowers, T. A. (1977). Candidate advertising: The agenda is the message. In D. L. Shaw & M. E. McCombs (Eds.), *The emergence of American public issues: The agenda-setting function of the press* (pp. 53-67). St. Paul, MN: West.

Boyer, P. J. (1986). Famine in Ethiopia: The TV accident that exploded. In M. Emery & T. C. Smythe (Eds.), *Readings in mass communication: Concepts and issues in the mass media* (pp. 293-298). Dubuque, IA: William C. Brown.

Brecher, M., Steinberg, B., & Stein, J. (1969). A framework for research on foreign policy behavior. *Journal of Conflict Resolution, 13*(1), 75-101.

Brewer, D. M. (1993). *Media effects on policy agendas: The San Antonio Light's agenda "for the children."* Master's thesis, University of Texas, Austin.

Brosius, H., & Kepplinger, H. M. (1990). The agenda-setting function of television news: Static and dynamic views. *Communication Research, 17*(2), 183-211.

Brosius, H., & Kepplinger, H. M. (1992a). Linear and non linear models of agenda setting in television. *Journal of Broadcasting and Electronic Media, 36,* 5-32.

Brosius, H., & Kepplinger, H. M. (1992b, May). *In search of killer issues: Issue competition in the agenda-setting process.* Paper presented at the American Association for Public Opinion Research, St. Petersburg, FL.

Brosius, H., & Kepplinger, H. M. (1992c). Beyond agenda-setting: The influence of partisanship and television reporting on the electorate's voting intentions. *Journalism Quarterly, 69*(4), 893-901.

Brosius, H., & Weiman, G. (1996). *The media or the public: Who sets the agenda? A contribution to the notion of two-step flow of agenda-setting.* Paper presented to the International Communication Association, Chicago.

Brown, W. J., & Basil, M. D. (1993). *Impact of the "Magic Johnson" news story on AIDS prevention.* Paper presented at the International Communication Association, Washington, DC.

Brown, W. J., & Vincent, R. C. (1993). *The arms for hostages controversy: Media portrayals of U.S.-Iran policy.* Unpublished paper, Regent University, Virginia Beach, VA, College of Communication and the Arts.

Burd, G. (1991). A critique of two decades of agenda-setting research. In D. E. Protess & M. McCombs (Eds.), *Agenda-setting: Readings on media, public opinion, and policymaking* (pp. 291-294). Hillsdale, NJ: Lawrence Erlbaum.

Burdach, K. J. (1988). Reporting on deaths: The perspective coverage of accident news in a German tabloid. *European Journal of Communication, 3,* 81-89.

Campbell, J. C. (1990). The mass media, policy change, and Japanese old people [in Japanese]. *Leviathan: The Japanese Journal of Political Science, 7,* 49-74.

Carey, J. (1976). How media shape campaigns. *Journal of Communication, 26*(2), 50-57.

112

Carragee, K., Rosenblatt, M., & Michaud, G. (1987). Agenda-setting research: A critique and theoretical alternative. In S. Thomas (Ed.), *Studies in communication 3* (pp. 35-49). Norwood, NJ: Ablex.

Carter, R. F., Stamm, K. R., & Heintz-Knowles, K. (1992). Agenda-setting and consequentiality. *Journalism Quarterly, 69*(4), 868-877.

Caspi, D. (1982). The agenda-setting function of the Israeli press. *Knowledge: Creation, Diffusion, Utilization, 3*(3), 401-414.

Chaffee, S. H., & Izcaray, F. (1975). Mass communication functions in a media rich developing society. In S. H. Chaffee (Ed.), *Political communication: Issues and strategies for research* (pp. 367-395). Beverly Hills, CA: Sage.

Chaffee, S. H., & Wilson, D. G. (1977). Media rich, media poor: Two studies of diversity in agenda-holding. *Journalism Quarterly, 54,* 468-476.

Chang, T. (1989). The impact of presidential statements on press editorials regarding U.S. China policy, 1950-1984. *Communication Research, 16*(4), 486-509.

Cherry, D. (1986). *A longitudinal analysis of the agenda-setting power of the black periodical press.* Unpublished doctoral dissertation, University of North Carolina, Chapel Hill.

Cobb, R. W., & Elder, C. D. (1971). The politics of agenda building: An alternative perspective for modern democratic theory. *Journal of Politics, 33,* 892-915.

Cobb, R. W., & Elder, C. D. (1981). Communication and public policy. In D. D. Nimmo & K. R. Sanders (Eds.), *Handbook of political communication* (pp. 391-416). Beverly Hills, CA: Sage.

Cobb, R. W., & Elder, C. D. (1983). *Participation in American politics: The dynamics of agenda-building.* Boston: Allyn & Bacon; Baltimore: Johns Hopkins University Press. (Original work published 1972)

Cobb, R. W., Ross, J., & Ross, M. H. (1976). Agenda-building as a comparative political process. *American Political Science Review, 70,* 126-138.

Cohen, A. A. (1976). Radio vs. TV: The effect of the medium. *Journal of Communication, 26,* 29-35.

Cohen, B. C. (1963). *The press and foreign policy.* Princeton, NJ: Princeton University Press.

Cohen, B. C. (1965). *Foreign policy in American government.* Boston: Little, Brown.

Cohen, B. C. (1967). Mass communication and foreign policy. In J. N. Rosenau (Ed.), *Domestic sources of foreign policy* (pp. 195-212). New York: Free Press.

Cohen, B. C. (1970). The relationship between public opinion and foreign policy makers. In M. Small (Ed.), *Public opinion and historians* (pp. 65-80). Detroit, MI: Wayne State University Press.

Cohen, B. C. (1983). *The public's impact on foreign policy.* Lanham, MD: University Press of America.

Cook, F. L., & Skogan, W. G. (1990). Agenda-setting and the rise and fall of policy issues. *Government and Politics, 8,* 395-415.

Cook, F. L., & Skogan, W. G. (1991). Agenda-setting: Convergent and divergent voice models of the rise and fall of policy issues. In *Agenda-setting: Readings on media, public opinion and policymaking* (pp. 189-206). Hillsdale, NJ: Lawrence Erlbaum.

Cook, F. L., Tyler, T. R., Goetz, E. J., Protess, D. L., Leff, D. R., & Molotch, H. L. (1983). Media and agenda-setting: Effects on the public, interest group leaders, policy makers and policy. *Public Opinion Quarterly, 47*(1), 16-35.

Cook, T. E., & Colby, D. C. (1991). The mass-mediated epidemic: The politics of AIDS on the nightly network news. In E. Fee & D. M. Fox (Eds.), *AIDS: The making of a chronic disease* (pp. 84-122). Berkeley: University of California Press.

Coombs, S. L. (1981). Dynamics in agenda-setting. In M. B. MacKuen & S. L. Coombs (Eds.), *More than news: Media power in public affairs.* Beverly Hills, CA: Sage.

Crenson, M. A. (1971). *The un-politics of air pollution: A study of non-decision making in two cities.* Baltimore, MD: Johns Hopkins University Press.

Danielian, L., & Reese, S. (1989). A closer look at intermedia influences on agenda-setting: The cocaine issue of 1986. In P. J. Shoemaker (Ed.), *Communication campaigns about drugs: Government, media and the public* (pp. 47-64). Hillsdale, NJ: Lawrence Erlbaum.

Davis, F. J. (1952). Crime news in Colorado newspapers. *American Journal of Sociology, 57,* 325-330.

Dearing, J. W. (1989). Setting the polling agenda for the issue of AIDS. *Public Opinion Quarterly, 53*(3), 309-329.

Dearing, J. W. (1992). Foreign blood and domestic politics: The issue of AIDS in Japan. In E. Fee & D. M. Fox (Eds.), *AIDS: The making of a chronic disease* (pp. 326-345). Berkeley: University of California Press.

Dearing, J. W., & Rogers, E. M. (1992). AIDS and the media agenda. In T. Edgar, M. Fitzpatrick, & V. Freimuth (Eds.), *AIDS: A communication perspective* (pp. 173-194). Hillsdale, NJ: Lawrence Erlbaum.

DeFleur, M. L. (1987). The growth and decline of research on the diffusion of the news 1945-1985. *Communication Research, 14*(1), 109-130.

DeGeorge, W. F. (1981). Conceptualization and measurement of audience agenda. In G. C. Wilhoit & H. DeBeck (Eds.), *Mass communication review yearbook 2* (pp. 291-222). Beverly Hills, CA: Sage.

Demers, D. P., Craff, D., Choi, Y., & Pessin, B. M. (1989). Issue obtrusiveness and the agenda-setting effects of national network news. *Communication Research, 16*(6), 793-812.

Derksen, L., & Gartrell, J. (1993). The social context of recycling. *American Sociological Review, 58,* 434-442.

Donohew, L., Helm, D., & Haas, J. (1989). Drugs and (Len) Bias on the sport page. In L. A. Wenner (Ed.), *Media, sports, and society* (pp. 225-237). Newbury Park, CA: Sage.

Downs, A. (1972). Up and down with ecology: The issue-attention cycle. *Public Interest, 28,* 38-50.

Eaton, H., Jr. (1990). Agenda-setting with bi-weekly data on content of three national media. *Journalism Quarterly, 67,* 942-948.

Edelstein, A. S. (1983). Communication and culture: The value of comparative studies. *Journal of Communication, 33*(3), 302-310.

Edelstein, A. S. (1993). Thinking about the criterion variable in agenda-setting research. *Journal of Communication, 43*(2), 85-99.

Edelstein, A. S., Ito, Y., & Kepplinger, H. M. (1989). Agenda-setting in the multicultural context. In *Communication and culture: A comparative approach* (pp. 224-255). New York: Longman.

Eichhorn, W. (1993, August). *An experimental test of the agenda-setting function of the press.* Paper presented at the Association for Education in Journalism and Mass Communication, Kansas City.

Einsiedel, E. F., Salomone, K. L., & Schneider, F. P. (1984). Crime: Effects of media exposure and personal experience on issue salience. *Journalism Quarterly, 61,* 131-136.

114

Entman, R. M. (1989). How the media affect what people think: An information processing approach. *Journal of Politics, 51,* 347-370.

Erbring, L., Goldenberg, E. N., & Miller, A. H. (1980). Front-page news and real-world cues: A new look at agenda-setting by the media. *American Journal of Political Science, 24*(1), 16-49.

Erikson, R. S. (1976). The relationship between public opinion and state policy: A new look based on some forgotten data. *American Journal of Political Science, 20,* 25-36.

Erikson, R. S. (1978). Constituency opinion and congressional behavior: A re-examination of the Miller-Stokes representation data. *American Journal of Political Science, 22,* 511-535.

Erikson, R. S., Wright, G. C., & McIver, J. P. (1993). *Statehouse democracy: Public opinion and policy in the American states.* New York: Cambridge University Press.

Ettema, J. S., Protess, D. L., Leff, D. R., Miller, P. V., Doppelt, J., & Cook, F. L. (1991). Agenda-setting as politics: A case study of the press-public-policy connection. *Communication, 12,* 75-98.

Eyal, C. H. (1979). *Time-frame in agenda setting research: A study of the conceptual and methodological factors affecting the time frame context of the agenda-setting process.* Unpublished doctoral dissertation, Syracuse University, Syracuse, NY.

Eyal, C. H. (1981). The roles of newspapers and television in agenda-setting. In G. C. Wilhoit & H. DeBock (Eds.), *Mass communication review yearbook 2* (pp. 225-234). Beverly Hills, CA: Sage.

Eyal, C., Winter, J. P., & DeGeorge, W. F. (1981). The concept of time frame in agenda-setting. In G. C. Wilhoit & H. DeBock (Eds.), *Mass communication review yearbook 2* (pp. 212-218). Beverly Hills, CA: Sage.

Eyal, C. H., Winter, J. P., & McCombs, M. E. (1980). The agenda-setting role of mass communication. In M. Emery & T. C. Smythe (Eds.), *Reading in mass communication: Concepts and issues in the mass media* (pp. 15-20). Dubuque, IA: William C. Brown.

Eyestone, R. (1974). *From social issues to public policy.* New York: Wiley.

Fan, D. P., & Norem, L. (1991, May). *The media and the fate of the Medicare Catastrophic Coverage Act.* Paper presented at the International Communication Association, Chicago.

Fancher, M. J. (1993, August). *Media agenda-setting and the United States Supreme Court's civil liberties docket, 1981-1990.* Paper presented at the Association for Education and Mass Communication, Kansas City.

Fields, J. M., & Schuman, H. (1976). Public beliefs about the beliefs of the public. *Public Opinion Quarterly, 40,* 427-448.

Fishman, M. (1978). Crime waves as ideology. *Social Problems, 25,* 531-543.

Fryling, A. C. (1985). *Setting the congressional agenda: Public opinion in a media age.* Unpublished doctoral dissertation, Massachusetts Institute of Technology, Cambridge.

Funkhouser, G. R. (1973a). The issues of the sixties: An exploratory study in the dynamics of public opinion. *Public Opinion Quarterly, 37*(1), 62-75.

Funkhouser, G. R. (1973b). Trends in media coverage of the issues of the sixties. *Journalism Quarterly, 50,* 533-538.

Gaddy, G. D., & Tanjong, E. (1986). Earthquake coverage by the Western press. *Journal of Communication, 36,* 105-112.

Gadir, S. (1982). Media agenda-setting in Australia: The rise and fall of public issues. *Media Information Australia, 26,* 13-23.

Gadziala, S. M., & Becker, L. B. (1983). A new look at agenda-setting in the 1976 election campaign. *Journalism Quarterly, 60*(1), 122-126.

Gamson, W. A. (1975). *The strategy of protest*. Homewood, IL: Dorsey.

Gamson, W. A. (1992). *Talking politics*. Cambridge: Cambridge University Press.

Gamson, W. A., & Modigliani, A. (1989). Media discourse and public opinion on nuclear power: A constructionist approach. *American Journal of Science, 95*(1), 1-37.

Gandy, O. (1982). *Beyond agenda-setting: Information subsidies and public policy.* Norwood, NJ: Ablex.

Gans, H. J. (1979). *Deciding what's news: A study of CBS Evening News, NBC Nightly News, Newsweek and Time.* New York: Pantheon.

Gantz, W., & Greenberg, B. S. (1990). The role of informative television programs in the battle against AIDS. *Health Communication, 2*(4), 199-215.

Gaziano, C. (1985). Neighborhood newspapers and neighborhood leaders: Influences on agenda setting and definitions of issues. *Communication Research, 12*(4), 568-594.

Gellert, G. A., Weismuller, P. C., Higgins, K. V., & Maxwell, R. M. (1992). Disclosure of AIDS in celebrities. *New England Journal of Medicine, 327*(19), 1389.

Gerstlé, J., Davis, D. K., & Duhamel, O. (1991). Television news and the construction of political reality in France and the United States. In L. L. Kaid, J. Gerstlé, & K. R. Sanders (Eds.), *Mediated politics in two cultures: Presidential campaigning in the United States and France.* New York: Praeger.

Gilbert, S., Eyal, C., McCombs, M. E., & Nicholas, D. (1980). The State of the Union Address and the press agenda. *Journalism Quarterly, 57*(4), 584-588.

Gilljam, M. (1984). Pluralist and Marxist agenda-setting research: The possibilities for a convergence between tradition. *Gazette, 34*, 77-90.

Goodman, R. (1994, May). *Bush administration congressional versus presidential agenda-setting: The China most favored nation controversy.* Paper presented at the International Communication Association, Albuquerque.

Gordon, M. T., & Heath, L. (1991). The news business, crime, and fear. In D. L. Protess & M. McCombs (Eds.), *Agenda-setting: Readings on media, public opinion, and policy making* (pp. 71-74). Hillsdale, NJ: Lawrence Erlbaum.

Gormley, W. T., Jr. (1975). Newspaper agenda and political elites. *Journalism Quarterly, 52*, 304-308.

Graham, T. W. (1988, May). *International control of atomic energy: Forging the cold-war consensus, 1945-1950.* Paper presented at the American Association of Public Opinion Research, Toronto.

Grunig, J. E., & Ipes, D. A. (1983). The anatomy of a campaign against drunk driving. *Public Relations Review, 9*, 36-52.

Haney, R. D. (1993). Agenda-setting during the Persian Gulf crisis. In B. S. Greenberg & W. Gantz (Eds.), *Desert Storm and the mass media* (pp. 113-124). Cresskill, NJ: Hampton.

Hauser, J. R. (1986). Agendas and consumer choice. *Journal of Marketing Research, 23*, 199-212.

Heclo, H. (1978). Issue networks and the executive establishment. In A. King (Ed.), *The new American political system* (pp. 87-124). Washington, DC: American Enterprise Institute.

Heeter, C., Brown, N., Soffin, S., Stanley, C., & Salwen, M. (1989). Agenda-setting by electronic text news. *Journalism Quarterly, 66*, 101-106.

Hertog, J. K., Finnegan, J. R., Jr., & Kahn, E. (1994). Media coverage of AIDS, cancer, and sexually transmitted diseases: A test of the public arenas model. *Journalism Quarterly, 71*(2), 291-304.

Hibbs, D. A., Jr. (1979). The mass public and macroeconomic performance: The dynamics of public opinion toward unemployment and inflation. *American Journal of Political Science, 23*(4), 705-731.

Hibbs, M. P. (1993). *A crossfire of information: A network approach to the agenda-setting hypothesis of the press: The case of steel trade.* Unpublished doctoral dissertation, University of Illinois, Chicago.

Hilgartner, S., & Bosk, C. L. (1988). The rise and fall of social problems: A public arenas model. *American Journal of Sociology, 94*(1), 53-78.

Hill, D. B. (1985). Viewer characteristics and agenda-setting by television news. *Public Opinion Quarterly, 49*(3), 340-350.

Holaday, D., & Kuo, E. (1992, August). *Upsetting the agenda: Media and the 1991 Singapore election.* Paper presented at the Association for Education in Journalism and Mass Communication, Montreal.

Horie, H. (1982). Taishu-Shakai to Masu-Demokurashi [Mass society and mass democracy]. In H. Horie et al. (Eds.), *Gendai no Seiji to Shakai* (pp. 30-42). Tokyo: Hokuju Shuppan.

Hubbard, J. C., DeFleur, M. L., & DeFleur, L. B. (1975). Mass media influences on public conceptions of social problems. *Social Problems, 23*, 22-34.

Ishikawa, M. (1990). Media's impact: "To the powers that be" to "from the powers that be" [in Japanese]. *Leviathan: The Japanese Journal of Political Science, 7*, 30-48.

Iwabuchi, Y. (1986). Masu-Media no Joho to Soten-Sentaku [Mass media information and issue choice]. In H. Horie & M. Umamura (Eds.), *Tohyo-Kodo to Seiji-ishiki* (pp. 181-195). Tokyo: Keio-Tsushin.

Iwabuchi, Y. (1989). Soten-Hodo to Soten-Sentaku [A study of agenda-setting in the 1986 election]. *Shimbun-Kenkyujo Nempo, 33*, 75-94 (Institute for Communication, Keio University).

Iyengar, S. (1979). Television news and issue salience: A re-examination of the agenda-setting hypothesis. *American Politics Quarterly, 7*, 395-416.

Iyengar, S. (1987). Television news and citizen's explanations of national affairs. *American Political Science Review, 81*(3), 815-831.

Iyengar, S. (1988). New directions of agenda-setting research. In J. Anderson (Ed.), *Communication yearbook 11* (pp. 595-602). Newbury Park, CA: Sage.

Iyengar, S. (1990). The accessibility bias in politics: Television news and public opinion. *International Journal of Public Opinion Research, 2*(1), 1-15.

Iyengar, S. (1991). *Is anyone responsible? How television frames political issues.* Chicago: University of Chicago Press.

Iyengar, S., & Kinder, D. R. (1985). Psychological accounts of media agenda-setting. In S. Kraus & R. M. Perloff (Eds.), *Mass media and political thought* (pp. 117-140). Beverly Hills, CA: Sage.

Iyengar, S., & Kinder, D. R. (1986). More than meet the eye: TV news, priming, and public evaluations of the president. In G. Comstock (Ed.), *Public communication and behavior 1* (pp. 135-171). New York: Academic Press.

Iyengar, S., & Kinder, D. R. (1987). *News that matters: Television and American opinion.* Chicago: University of Chicago Press.

Iyengar, S., Peters, M. D., & Kinder, D. R. (1982). Experimental demonstrations of the 'not-so-minimal' consequences of television news programs. *American Political Science Review, 76*(4), 848-858.

Iyengar, S., Peters, M. P., Kinder, D. R., & Krosnick, J. A. (1984). The evening news and presidential evaluations. *Journal of Personality and Social Psychology, 46*, 778-787.

Iyengar, S., & Simon, A. (1993). News coverage of the Gulf crisis and public opinion: A survey of effects. *Communication Research, 20*(3), 365-383.

Johnson, T. J., & Wanta, W. (1994, August). *Influence dealers: A path analysis model of agenda-building during Richard Nixon's War on Drugs.* Paper presented at the Association for Education in Journalism and Mass Communication, Atlanta.

Junack, M. E., McCombs, M. E., & Shaw, D. L. (1977). Using polls and content analysis to study an election. In D. L. Shaw & M. E. McCombs (Eds.), *The emergence of American public issues: The agenda-setting function of the press* (pp. 157-169). St. Paul, MN: West.

Kaid, L. L., Hale, K., & Williams, J. (1977). Media agenda-setting of a specific political event. *Journalism Quarterly, 54,* 584-587.

Kanervo, E. W., & Kanervo, D. W. (1989). How town administrators' view relates to agenda-building in community press. *Journalism Quarterly, 66*(2), 308-315.

Keohane, R. O., & Nye, J. S. (1977). *Power and interdependence: World politics in transition.* Boston: Little, Brown.

Kepplinger, H. M., & Roth, H. (1979). Creating a crisis: German mass media and oil supply in 1973-74. *Public Opinion Quarterly, 43,* 285-296.

Kerr, P. (1986, November 17). Anatomy of an issue: Drugs, the evidence, the reaction. *New York Times,* pp. 1, 12.

Kim, J. K., Shoar-Ghaffari, P., & Gustainis, J. J. (1990). Agenda-setting functions of a media event: The case of 'Amerika'. *Political Communication and Persuasion, 7,* 1-10.

Kingdon, J. W. (1984). *Agendas, alternatives, and public policies.* Boston: Little, Brown.

Kobayashi, Y. (1990). Mass media and political attitudes in Japan [in Japanese]. *Leviathan: The Japanese Journal of Political Science, 7,* 97-114.

Kojima, K. (1982). Seiji-Katei to Masu-Kommyunikeishon [Political process and mass communication]. In I. Takeuchi & K. Kojima (Eds.), *Gendai Masu-Kommyunikeishon-Ron* (pp. 218-245). Tokyo: Yuhikaku.

Kosicki, G. (1993). Problems and opportunities in agenda-setting research. *Journal of Communication, 43*(2), 100-127.

Kovanik, B. (1994, August). *Agenda-setting in the 1924-1926 public health controversy over ethyl (leaded) gasoline.* Paper presented at the Association for Education in Journalism and Mass Communication, Atlanta.

Kraus, S. (1985). The studies and the world outside. In S. Kraus & R. M. Perloff (Eds.), *Mass media and political thought.* Beverly Hills, CA: Sage.

Lambeth, E. B. (1978). Perceived influence of the press on energy policy making. *Journalism Quarterly, 72,* 11-18.

Lang, G. E., & Lang, K. (1981). Watergate: An exploration of the agenda-building process. In G. C. Wilhoit & H. DeBock (Eds.), *Mass communication review yearbook 2* (pp. 447-468). Beverly Hills, CA: Sage.

Lang, G. E., & Lang, K. (1983). *The battle for public opinion: The president, the press and the polls during Watergate.* New York: Columbia University Press.

Lasswell, H. D. (1927). *Propaganda technique in the world war.* New York: Knopf.

Lasswell, H. D. (1948). The structure and function of communication in society. In L. Bryson (Ed.), *The communication of ideas: A series of addresses.* New York: Harper.

Lazarsfeld, P. F., & Merton, R. K. (1964). Mass communication, popular taste and organized social action. In L. Bryson (Ed.), *The communication of ideas: A series of addresses* (pp. 95-118). New York: Harper. (Original work published 1948)

Leff, D., Protess, D., & Brooks, S. C. (1986). Crusading journalism: Changing public attitudes and policy-making agenda. *Public Opinion Quarterly, 50,* 300-315.

118

Linsky, M. (1986). *How the press affects federal policy making*. New York: Norton.
Linsky, M., Moore, J., O'Donnell, W., & Whitman, D. (1986). *How the press affects federal policy-making: Six cases studies*. New York: Norton.
Lippmann, W. (1922). *Public opinion*. New York: Harcourt Brace.
Lipsky, M. (1968). Protest as a political resource. *American Political Science Review, 62*, 1144-1158.
Lowery, S., & DeFleur, M. L. (1987). *Milestones in mass communication research: Media effects*. New York: Longman.
Lowi, T. J. (1964). American business, public policy, case studies and political theory. *World Politics, 16*(4), 677-715.
MacKuen, M. B. (1981). Social communication and the mass policy agenda. In M. B. MacKuen & S. L. Coombs (Eds.), *More than news: Media power in public affairs* (pp. 19-144). Beverly Hills, CA: Sage.
MacKuen, M. B., & Coombs, S. L. (1981). *More than news: Media power in public affairs*. Beverly Hills, CA: Sage.
Maeda, T. (1978). Kodokushi to Seiji-Ishiki [Newspaper subscription and political consciousness]. *Hogaku-Kenkyu, 51*(5), 311-338 (Keio University).
Major, A., & Atwood, L. E. (1991). U.S. newsmagazine coverage of the U.S. and French presidential elections: Mediated constructions of the candidates and the issues. In *Mediated politics in two cultures: Presidential campaigning in the United States and France*. New York: Praeger.
Manheim, J. B. (1986). A model of agenda dynamics. In M. L. McLaughlin (Ed.), *Communication yearbook 10* (pp. 499-516). Beverly Hills, CA: Sage.
Manheim, J. B., & Albritton, R. B. (1984). Changing national images: International public relations and media agenda-setting. *American Political Science Review, 73*, 641-647.
Mansbach, R. W., & Vasquez, J. A. (1981). *In search of theory: A new paradigm for global politics*. New York: Columbia University Press.
Mathes, R., & Pfetsch, B. (1991). The role of the alternative press in the agenda-building process: Spill-over effects and media opinion leadership. *European Journal of Communication, 6*(1), 33-62.
Mayer, M. E., Gudykunst, W. B., Perrill, N. K., & Merrill, B. D. (1986). *Diffusion of information about the shuttle explosion* (Working paper). Tempe: Arizona State University, Communication Research Center, Department of Communication.
Mayer, R. N. (1991). Gone yesterday, here today: Consumer issues in the agenda-setting process. *Journal of Social Issues, 47*(1), 21-39.
Mazur, A. (1981). Media coverage and public opinion on scientific controversies. *Journal of Communication, 31*, 106-115.
Mazur, A. (1982). Bomb threats and the mass media. *American Sociological Review, 47*, 407-411.
Mazur, A. (1987). Putting radon on the public's risk agenda. *Science, Technology and Human Values, 12*(3-4), 86-93.
Mazur, A. (1990). Nuclear power, chemical hazards, and the quantity of reporting. *Minerva, 28*, 294-323.
Mazur, A., & Lee, J. (1993). Sounding the global alarm: Environmental issues in the U.S. national news. *Social Studies of Science, 23*, 681-720.
Mazza, M. (1987). *Agenda-setting effects of news media of perceived salience of unobtrusive and obtrusive issues over time*. Master's thesis, University of Connecticut, Storrs.
McCarthy, J. D., & Zald, M. N. (1977). Resource mobilization and social movements: A partial theory. *American Journal of Sociology, 82*(6), 1212-1241.

119

McCauley, M. P., & Frederick, E. R. (1993, August). *The War on Drugs: A construc-tionalist view.* Paper presented at the Association for Education in Journal-ism and Mass Communication, Kansas City.

McClure, R. D., & Patterson, T. D. (1976). Print vs. network news. *Journal of Communication, 26,* 23-28.

McCombs, M. E. (1976). Agenda-setting research: A bibliographic essay. *Political Communication Review, 1,* 1-7.

McCombs, M. E. (1977). Newspaper vs. television: Mass communication effects across time. In D. L. Shaw & M. E. McCombs (Eds.), *The emergence of American political issues: The agenda-setting function of the press* (pp. 89-105). St. Paul, MN: West.

McCombs, M. E. (1981a). The agenda-setting approach. In D. D. Sidney & K. R. Sidney (Eds.), *Handbook of political communication* (pp. 121-140). Beverly Hills, CA: Sage.

McCombs, M. E. (1981b). Setting the agenda for agenda-setting research: An as-sessment of the priority, ideas and problems. In G. C. Wilhoit & H. DeBock (Eds.), *Mass communication review yearbook 2* (pp. 219-224). Beverly Hills, CA: Sage.

McCombs, M. E. (1992). Explorers and surveyors: Expanding strategies for agenda-setting research. *Journalism Quarterly, 69*(4), 813-824.

McCombs, M. E., & Gilbert, S. (1986). News influences on our pictures of the world. In J. Bryant & D. Zillman (Eds.), *Perspectives on media effects* (pp. 1-15). Hillsdale, NJ: Lawrence Erlbaum.

McCombs, M. E., & Mazel-Waters, L. (1976). Agenda-setting: A new perspective on mass communication. *Mass Communication Review, 3,* 3-7.

McCombs, M. E., & Shaw, D. L. (1972). The agenda-setting function of the mass media. *Public Opinion Quarterly, 36,* 176-187.

McCombs, M. E., & Shaw, D. L. (1976). Structuring the unseen environment. *Journal of Communication, 26*(2), 18-22.

McCombs, M. E., & Shaw, D. L. (1977). Agenda-setting and the political process. In D. L. Shaw & M. E. McCombs (Eds.), *The emergence of American political is-sues: The agenda-setting function of the press* (pp. 149-156). St. Paul, MN: West.

McCombs, M. E., & Shaw, D. L. (1993). The evolution of agenda-setting research: Twenty-five years in the marketplace. *Journal of Communication, 43*(2), 58-67.

McCombs, M. E., & Weaver, D. H. (1985). Toward a merger of gratification and agenda-setting research. In K. E. Rosengren, L. A. Wenner, & P. Palmgreen (Eds.), *Media gratifications research: Current perspectives* (pp. 95-108). Beverly Hills, CA: Sage.

McCombs, M., & Zhu, J. (1995). Capacity, diversity, and volatility of the public agenda: Trends from 1954 to 1994. *Public Opinion Quarterly, 59*(4), 495-535.

McKean, D. (1992). *Media coverage of the drug crisis* (Forum Report). Washington, DC: Annenberg Washington Program.

McLeod, J. M., Becker, L. B., & Byrnes, J. E. (1974). Another look at the agenda-setting function of the press. *Communication Research, 1,* 131-166.

McLeod, J. M., Becker, L. B., & Byrnes, J. E. (1981). Mass communication and voter volatility. *Public Opinion Quarterly, 45*(1), 69-90.

McLeod, J. M., Se-Wen, S., Chi, H., & Pan, Z. (1990, August). *Metaphor and the media: What shapes public understanding of the "War" Against Drugs?* Paper presented at the Association for Education in Journalism and Mass Com-munication, Minneapolis.

McLuskie, E. (1992). The mediacentric agenda of agenda-setting research: Eclipse of the public sphere. In S. A. Deetz (Ed.), *Communication yearbook 15* (pp. 410-424). Newbury Park, CA: Sage.

Mead, T. D. (1994). The daily newspaper as political agenda setter: *The Charlotte Observer* and metropolitan reform. *State and Local Government Review, 26*(1), 27-37.

Megwa, E. R., & Brenner, D. J. (1988). Toward a paradigm of media agenda-setting effect: Agenda-setting as a process. *Howard Journal of Communication, 1*(1), 39-56.

Mikami, S., Takeshita, T., Nakada, M., & Kawabata, M. (1994, July). *The media coverage and public awareness of environmental issues in Japan.* Paper presented at the International Association for Mass Communication Research, Seoul.

Miller, A. H., Goldenberg, E. N., & Erbring, L. (1979). Type-set politics: Impact of newspapers on public confidence. *American Political Science Review, 73*(1), 67-84.

Miller, J. D. (1987). *The impact of the Challenger accident on public attitude toward the space program.* Report to the National Science Foundation by the Public Opinion Laboratory, Northern Illinois University, Dekalb.

Miller, K. (1992). Smoking up a storm: Public relations and advertising in the contribution of the cigarette problem, 1983-1984. *Journalism Monographs, 136.*

Miller, S. H. (1978). Reporters and congressmen: Living in symbiosis. *Journalism Monographs, 53.*

Miller, W. E., & Stokes, D. E. (1963). The politics of agenda-building: An alternative perspective for modern democratic theory. *Journal of Politics, 33,* 892-915.

Missika, J., & Bregman, D. (1987). On framing the campaign: Mass media role in negotiating the meaning of the vote. *European Journal of Communication, 2*(3), 289-309.

Molotch, H. L., & Lester, M. (1974). News as purposive behavior: On the strategic use of routine events, accidents and scandals. *American Sociological Review, 39,* 101-112.

Molotch, H. L., Protess, D. L., & Gordon, M. T. (1987). The media-policy connection: Ecology of news. In D. Paletz (Ed.), *Political communication: Theories, cases and assessments* (pp. 26-48). Norwood, NJ: Ablex.

Monroe, A. D. (1979). Consistency between public preferences and national policy decisions. *American Politics Quarterly, 7*(1), 3-19.

Montgomery, K. C. (1989). *Target: Prime time—Advocacy groups and the struggle over entertainment television.* New York: Oxford University Press.

Montgomery, K. C. (1993). The Harvard Alcohol Project: Promoting the designated driver on television. In T. E. Backer & E. M. Rogers (Eds.), *Organizational aspects of health communication campaigns: What works?* (pp. 178-202). Newbury Park, CA: Sage.

Mullins, L. E. (1977). Agenda-setting and the young voter. In D. L. Shaw & M. E. McCombs (Eds.), *The emergence of American political issues: The agenda-setting function of the press* (pp. 133-148). St. Paul, MN: West.

Nelson, B. J. (1984). *Making an issue of child abuse: Political agenda setting for social problems.* Chicago: University of Chicago Press.

Nelson, B. J. (1991). Making an issue of child abuse. In D. L. Shaw & M. E. McCombs (Eds.), *Agenda-setting: Readings on media, public opinion and policymaking* (pp. 161-170). Hillsdale, NJ: Lawrence Erlbaum.

Neuman, W. R. (1990). The threshold of public attention. *Public Opinion Quarterly, 54,* 159-176.

Neuman, W. R., & Fryling, A. C. (1985). Patterns of political cognition: An exploration of the public mind. In S. Kraus & R. M. Perloff (Eds.), *Mass media and political thought: An information processing approach* (pp. 223-240). Beverly Hills, CA: Sage.

Neuman, W. R., Just, M. R., & Crigler, A. N. (1992). *Common knowledge: News and the construction of political meaning.* Chicago: University of Chicago Press.

Neville, J. F. (1990, August). *The Rosenbergs and the National Guardian: Cold war agenda-setting, 1951-1953.* Paper presented at the Association for Education in Journalism and Mass Communication, Minneapolis.

Nord, D. P. (1981). The politics of agenda setting in late 19th century cities. *Journalism Quarterly, 58,* 565-574, 612.

Okada, N. (1987). Ajenda-Settei Kenkyu no Gaikan to Kadai [A review and research agenda of agenda-setting research]. In M. Mita & T. Miyajima (Eds.), *Bunka to Gendai Shakai* (pp. 175-207). Tokyo: University of Tokyo Press.

O'Keefe, G. J., & Reid-Nash, K. (1987). Crime news and real-world blues: The effects of the media on social reality. *Communication Research, 14*(2), 147-163.

Page, B. I., & Shapiro, R. Y. (1983). Effects of public opinion on policy. *American Political Science Review, 77,* 175-190.

Page, B. I., Shapiro, R. Y., & Dempsey, G. R. (1987). What moves public opinion? *American Political Science Review, 81*(1), 23-43.

Palmgreen, P., & Clarke, P. (1977). Agenda-setting with local and national issues. *Communication Research, 14,* 435-452.

Park, R. E. (1922). *The immigrant press and its control.* New York: Harper.

Pertschuk, M. (1987). The role of public interest groups in setting the public agenda for the '90s. *Journal of Consumer Affairs, 21*(2), 171-182.

Peterson, S. (1972). Events, mass opinion, and elite attitudes. In R. L. Merritt (Ed.), *Communication in international politics* (pp. 252-271). Urbana: University of Illinois Press.

Piotrow, P. T. (1973). *Public ambiguity and government nonpolicy: World population crisis: The United States response.* New York: Praeger.

Ploughman, P. (1984). *The creation of newsworthy events: An analysis of newspaper coverage of the man-made disaster at Love Canal.* Unpublished doctoral dissertation, State University of New York, Buffalo.

Pollack, J. C., Robinson, J. L., Jr., & Murray, M. C. (1973). Media agendas and human rights: The Supreme Court decision on abortion. *Journalism Quarterly, 55*(3), 544-569.

Pritchard, D. (1987). Homicide and bargained justice: The agenda-setting effect of crime news on prosecutors. In M. Gurevitch & M. R. Levy (Eds.), *Mass communication yearbook 6* (pp. 384-400). Newbury Park, CA: Sage.

Protess, D. L., Cook, F. L., Curtin, T. R., Gordon, M. T., Leff, D. R., McCombs, M. E., & Miller, P. (1987). The impact of investigative reporting on public opinion and policy making: Targeting toxic waste. *Public Opinion Quarterly, 51,* 166-185.

Protess, D. L., Cook, F. L., Doppelt, J. C., Ettema, J. S., Gordon, M. T., Leff, D. R., & Miller, P. (1991). *The journalism of outrage.* New York: Guilford.

Protess, D. L., Leff, D. R., Brooks, S. C., & Gordon, M. T. (1985). Uncovering rape: The watchdog press and the limits of agenda-setting. *Public Opinion Quarterly, 49*(1), 19-37.

Protess, D. L., & McCombs, M. E. (1991). *Agenda-setting: Readings on media, public opinion and policymaking.* Hillsdale, NJ: Lawrence Erlbaum.

Rabinowitz, G., Prothro, J. W., & Jacoby, W. (1982). Salience as a factor in the impact of issues on candidate evaluation. *Journal of Politics, 44,* 41-63.

Ramaprasad, J. (1983). Agenda-setting: Is not a 1984 or is a 1984 view. *Gazette, 32,* 119-135.

122

Ramsey, M. (1992). *A newspaper campaign to place children's issues on the community agenda.* Master's thesis, University of Texas, Austin.

Reese, S. D. (1991). Setting the media's agenda: A power balance perspective. In J. A. Anderson (Ed.), *Communication yearbook 14* (pp. 309-340). Newbury Park, CA: Sage.

Reese, S. D., & Lucig, D. (1989). Intermedia influence and the drug issue: Converging on cocaine. In P. J. Shoemaker (Ed.), *Communication campaigns about drugs: Government, media and the public* (pp. 47-66). Hillsdale, NJ: Lawrence Erlbaum.

Reinarman, C. (1988). The social construction of an alcohol problem: The case of Mothers Against Drunk Drivers and social control in the 1980's. *Theory and Society, 17,* 91-120.

Roberts, M. (1992). Predicting voting behavior via the agenda-setting tradition. *Journalism Quarterly, 69*(4), 878-892.

Rogers, E. M., & Chang, S. (1991). Media coverage of technology issues: Ethiopian drought of 1984, AIDS, Challenger and Chernobyl. In L. Wilkens & P. Patterson (Eds.), *Risky business: Communicating issues of science, risk and public policy* (pp. 75-96). New York: Greenwood.

Rogers, E. M., & Dearing, J. W. (1988). Agenda-setting research: Where has it been? Where is it going? In J. A. Anderson (Ed.), *Communication yearbook 11* (pp. 555-594). Newbury Park, CA: Sage.

Rogers, E. M., Dearing, J. W., & Bregman, D. (1993). The anatomy of agenda-setting research. *Journal of Communication, 43*(2A), 68-84.

Rogers, E. M., Dearing, J. W., & Chang, S. (1991). AIDS in the 1980s: The agenda-setting process for a public issue. *Journalism Monographs, 126.*

Rogers, E. M., Dearing, J. W., & Liu, W. (1992, September). *Looking backward and forward at approaches to agenda-setting research.* Paper presented at the American Political Science Association, Chicago.

Rogers, E. M., McGilly, K., & McIntosh, K. M. (1990). Diffusion of innovations: How the environmental crisis got on the national agenda. In S. H. Broderick & L. B. Snyder (Eds.), *Proceedings of the Symposium on Volunteers and Communication in Natural Resource Education* (pp. 3-11). Storrs: University of Connecticut Cooperative Extension System.

Rosenau, J. N. (1961). *Public opinion and foreign policy.* New York: Random House.

Rosenau, J. N. (1971). Pre-theories and theories of foreign policy. In J. N. Rosenau (Ed.), *The scientific study of foreign policy.* New York: Free Press.

Salwen, M. B. (1985a). *An agenda for agenda-setting research: Problems in the paradigm.* Paper presented at the Speech Communication Association, San Juan, Puerto Rico.

Salwen, M. B. (1985b). *Agenda-setting with environmental issues: A study of time process, media dependency, audience salience, and newspaper reading.* Unpublished doctoral dissertation, Michigan State University, East Lansing.

Salwen, M. B. (1986, May). *Time in agenda-setting: The accumulation of media coverage on audience issue salience.* Paper presented at the International Communication Association, Chicago.

Salwen, M. B. (in press). News of Hurricane Andrew: The agenda of sources and the source's agenda. *Journalism Quarterly, 73.*

Salwen, M. B., & Matera, F. R. (1992). Public salience of foreign nations. *Journalism Quarterly, 69,* 623-632.

Sawicki, F., & Leland, C. M. (1991). The formation of the electoral agenda: A case study in social welfare issues in the United States and France. In *Mediated politics in two cultures: Presidential campaigning in the United States and France.* New York: Praeger.

123

Schattschneider, E. E. (1960). *The semisovereign people: A realist's view of democracy in America.* New York: Holt, Rinehart & Winston.

Schleuder, J., McCombs, M., & Wanta, W. (1991). Inside the agenda-setting process: How political advertising and TV news prime viewers to think about issues and candidates. In F. Biocca (Ed.), *Television and political advertising 1: Psychological processes* (pp. 263-310). Hillsdale, NJ: Lawrence Erlbaum.

Schmeling, D. G., & Wotring, C. E. (1976). Agenda-setting effects of drug abuse public service ads. *Journalism Quarterly, 54*(4), 743-746.

Schoenbach, K., & Semetko, H. A. (1992). Agenda-setting, agenda-reinforcing or agenda-deflating? A study of the 1990 German national election. *Journalism Quarterly, 69*(4), 837-846.

Schoenfeld, A. C. (1979). The press and NEPA: The case of the missing agenda. *Journalism Quarterly, 56*(3), 577-585.

Schoenfeld, A. C., Meier, R. F., & Griffin, R. J. (1979). Constructing a social problem: The press and the environment. *Social Problems, 27,* 38-61.

Schweitzer, J. C., & Smith, B. L. (1991, Summer). Community pressures on agenda-setting. *Newspaper Research Journal,* pp. 46-62.

Semetko, H., Blumler, J., Gurevitch, M., & Weaver, D. H. (1991). *The formation of campaign agendas: A comparative analysis of party and media roles in recent American and British elections.* Hillsdale, NJ: Lawrence Erlbaum.

Severin, W. J., & Tankard, J. W., Jr. (1992). Agenda setting. In W. J. Severin & J. W. Tankard, Jr. (Eds.), *Communication theories: Origins, methods, and uses in the mass media* (pp. 207-229). New York: Longman.

Shaw, D. L. (1977). The press agenda in a community setting. In D. L. Shaw & M. E. McCombs (Eds.), *The emergence of American political issues: The agenda-setting function of the press* (pp. 19-31). St. Paul, MN: West.

Shaw, D. L., & Clemmer, C. L. (1977). News and the public response. In D. L. Shaw & M. E. McCombs (Eds.), *The emergence of American political issues: The agenda-setting function of the press* (pp. 33-51). St. Paul, MN: West.

Shaw, D. L., & Martin, S. E. (1992). The function of mass media agenda setting. *Journalism Quarterly, 69*(4), 902-920.

Shaw, D. L., & McCombs, M. (1977). *The emergence of American political issues: The agenda-setting function of the press.* St. Paul, MN: West.

Shaw, D. L., & Slater, J. W. (1988). Press puts unemployment on agenda: Richmond Community Opinion, 1981-1984. *Journalism Quarterly, 65*(2), 407-411.

Shaw, E. F. (1977a). The interpersonal agenda. *The emergence of American political issues: The agenda-setting function of the press* (pp. 69-87). St. Paul, MN: West.

Shaw, E. F. (1977b). The agenda-setting hypothesis reconsidered: Interpersonal factors. *Gazette, 23,* 230-240.

Shaw, E. F. (1979). Agenda-setting and mass communication theory. *Gazette, 25*(2), 96-105.

Shefner, C. L., & Rogers, E. M. (1992, May). *Hollywood lobbyists: How social causes get in network television.* Paper presented at the International Communication Association, Miami.

Shoemaker, P. J. (Ed.). (1989). *Communication campaigns about drugs: Government, media, and the public.* Hillsdale, NJ: Lawrence Erlbaum.

Shoemaker, P. J., Danielian, L. H., & Brendlinger, N. (1991). Deviant acts, risky business and U.S. interests: The newsworthiness of world events. *Journalism Quarterly, 68*(4), 781-795.

Shoemaker, P. J., with Mayfield, E. K. (1987). Building a theory of news content: A synthesis of current approaches. *Journalism Monographs, 103.*

124

Shoemaker, P. J., Wanta, W., & Leggett, D. (1989). Drug coverage and public opinion, 1972-1986. In P. J. Shoemaker (Ed.), *Communication campaigns about drugs: Government, media and the public* (pp. 67-80). Hillsdale, NJ: Lawrence Erlbaum.

Siune, K., & Borre, O. (1975). Setting the agenda for a Danish election. *Journal of Communication, 25*(1), 65-73.

Smith, K. A. (1987a). Newspaper coverage and public concern about community issues: A time-series analysis. *Journalism Monographs, 101.*

Smith, K. A. (1987b). Effects of newspaper coverage on community issue concerns and local government evaluations. *Communication Research, 14*(4), 379-395.

Smith, K. A. (1988). Effects of coverage on neighborhood and community concerns. *Newspaper Research Journal, 9,* 35-47.

Smith, T. W. (1980). America's most important problem: A trend analysis, 1946-1976. *Public Opinion Quarterly, 44,* 164-180.

Soderlund, W. C., Waggenberg, R. H., Briggs, E. D., & Nelson, R. C. (1980). Regional and linguistic agenda-setting in Canada: A study of newspaper coverage of issues affecting political integration in 1976. *Canadian Journal of Political Science, 13*(2), 348-356.

Sohn, A. B. (1978). A longitudinal analysis of local non-political agenda-setting analysis. *Journalism Quarterly, 55,* 325-333.

Sohn, A. B. (1984). Newspaper agenda-setting and community expectations. *Journalism Quarterly, 61*(4), 892-896.

Stimson, J. A. (1976). Public support of American presidents: A cyclical model. *Public Opinion Quarterly, 40,* 1-21.

Stone, G. C., & McCombs, M. E. (1981). Tracing the time lag in agenda-setting. *Journalism Quarterly, 58*(1), 51-55.

Strodthoff, G. G., Hawkins, R. P., & Schoenfeld, A. C. (1985). Media roles in a social movement: A model of ideology diffusion. *Journalism Quarterly, 35*(2), 134-153.

Sutherland, M., & Galloway, J. (1981). Role of advertising: Persuasion or agenda-setting. *Journalism Quarterly, 58,* 51-55.

Swanson, D. L. (1988). Feeling the elephant: Some observations on agenda-setting research. *Communication yearbook 11* (pp. 603-619). Newbury Park, CA: Sage.

Swanson, L. L., & Swanson, D. L. (1978). The agenda-setting function of the first Ford-Carter debate. *Communication Monographs, 45,* 330-353.

Takeshita, T. (1981). Masu-Media no Gidai-Settei Kino [The agenda-setting function of mass media: Present state of research and associated problems]. *Shimbungaku Hyoron, 30,* 203-218.

Takeshita, T. (1983). Media Gidai-Settei Kasetsu No Jisshoteki-Kento [An empirical examination of the media agenda-setting hypothesis]. *Todai Shimbun-Kenkyujo Kiyo, 31,* 101-143 (Bulletin of the Institute of Journalism and Communication Studies, University of Tokyo).

Takeshita, T. (1984). Gidai-Settei Kenkyu no Shikaku [The perspective of agenda-setting research: Theory and verification in mass communication effects studies]. *Hosogaku Kankyu, 34,* 81-116.

Takeshita, T. (1988). Soten-Hodo to Gidai-Settei Kasetsu [Issue reporting and the agenda-setting hypothesis]. In Institute of Journalism and Communication Studies, University of Tokyo (Ed.), *Senkyo Hodo to Tohyo Kodo* (pp. 157-196). Tokyo: University of Tokyo Press.

Takeshita, T. (1990). On mass media and public opinion [in Japanese]. *Leviathan: The Japanese Journal of Political Science, 7,* 75-96.

125

Takeshita, T. (1992). Masu-Media ga Tsukuru Genjitsu-Ninshiki [The media as a constructor of our recognition of reality]. *Kagaku Asahi, 52*(12), 24-27.
Takeshita, T. (1993). Agenda-setting effects of the press in a Japanese local election. *Studies of Broadcasting, 29,* 194-216 (NHK).
Takeshita, T., & Mikami, S. (1995). How did the mass media influence the voter's choice in the 1993 general election in Japan? A study of agenda-setting. *Keio Communication Review, 17,* 27-41.
Takeuchi, I. (1982). Juyo-Katei No Kenkyu [The study of mass media uses and effects]. In I. Takeuchi & K. Kojima (Eds.), *Gendai Masu-Kommyunikeishon-ron* (pp. 44-79). Tokyo: Yuhikaku.
Tankard, J. W. (1990). Maxwell McCombs and agenda-setting. In W. D. Sloan (Ed.), *Makers of the media mind: Journalism educators and their ideas* (pp. 278-286). Hillsdale, NJ: Lawrence Erlbaum.
Tardy, C. H., Gaughan, B. J., Hemphill, M. R., & Crockett, N. (1981). Media agendas and political participation. *Journalism Quarterly, 58,* 15-22.
Tipton, L., Haney, R. D., & Baseheart, J. R. (1975). Media agenda-setting in city and state election campaigns. *Journalism Quarterly, 52*(1), 15-22.
Tokinoya, H. (1983). Gidai-Settei Riron ni yoru Kokoku-Koka no Kenkyu [Agenda-setting theory and advertising effects]. *16th Josei-Kenkyu-shu* (pp. 75-87). Tokyo: Yoshida Hideo Memorial Foundation.
Trumbo, C. (1995). Longitudinal modeling of public issues: An application of the agenda-setting process to the issue of global warming. *Journalism Monographs, 152.*
Tulving, E., & Schacter, D. L. (1990). Priming and human memory systems. *Science, 247,* 301-306.
Turk, V. (1986). Information subsidies and media content: A study of public relations influence on the news. *Journalism Monographs, 100.*
Walker, J. L. (1977). Setting the agenda in the U.S. Senate: A theory of problem selection. *British Journal of Political Science, 7,* 433-445.
Wallack, L. (1990). Two approaches to health promotion in the mass media. *World Health Forum, 11,* 143-164.
Wanta, W. (1986, August). *The agenda-setting effects of dominant photographs.* Paper presented at the Association for Education in Journalism and Mass Communication, Norman, OK.
Wanta, W. (1991). Presidential approval ratings as a variable in the agenda-building process. *Journalism Quarterly, 68*(4), 672-679.
Wanta, W., & Hu, Y. (1994). The effects of credibility, reliance, and exposure on media agenda-setting: A path analysis model. *Journalism Quarterly, 71*(1), 99-109.
Wanta, W., Hu, Y., & Miller, R. E. (1994). *Personal characteristics and susceptibility to media agenda-setting.* Paper presented at the International Communication Association, Sydney.
Wanta, W., & Mahmoud, M. (1990, August). *Obstacles to agenda-setting.* Paper presented at the Association for Education and Mass Communication, Minneapolis.
Wanta, W., & Miller, R. (1994, August). *Race as a variable in the agenda-setting process.* Paper presented at the Association for Education in Journalism and Mass Communication, Atlanta.
Wanta, W., & Newman, J. (1996). *Newspaper editors and the national agenda: The role of the gatekeepers in the agenda-setting process.* Paper presented at the International Communication Association, Chicago.

126

Wanta, W., Stephenson, M., Turk, J. V., & McCombs, M. E. (1989). How the president's State of the Union talk influenced news media agendas. *Journalism Quarterly, 66*(3), 537-541.

Wanta, W., & Wu, Y. (1992). Interpersonal communication and the agenda-setting process. *Journalism Quarterly, 69*(4), 847-855.

Watt, J. H., Jr., Mazza, M., & Snyder, L. (1993). Agenda-setting effects of television news coverage and the effects decay curve. *Communication Research, 20*(3), 408-435.

Watt, J. H., Jr., & van den Berg, S. (1981). How time dependency influences media effects in a community controversy. *Journalism Quarterly, 58*, 43-50.

Watts, L. (1994, August). *Medical researchers and media agenda-setters: Reporting cure research in newspapers, news magazines and network television news.* Paper presented at the Association for Education in Journalism and Mass Communication, Atlanta.

Weaver, D. H. (1977). Political issues and voter need for orientation. In D. L. Shaw & M. E. McCombs (Eds.), *The emergence of American political issues: The agenda-setting function of the press* (pp. 107-119). St. Paul, MN: West.

Weaver, D. H. (1984). Media agenda-setting and public opinion: Is there a link? In R. N. Bostrom (Ed.), *Communication yearbook 8* (pp. 680-691). Beverly Hills, CA: Sage.

Weaver, D. H. (1987). Media agenda-setting and elections: Assumptions and implications. In D. L. Paletz (Ed.), *Political communication research: Approaches, studies, assessments* (pp. 176-193). Norwood, NJ: Ablex.

Weaver, D. H., & Elliott, S. N. (1985). Who sets the agenda for the media? A study of local agenda-building. *Journalism Quarterly, 62*(1), 87-94.

Weaver, D. H., Graber, D. A., McCombs, M. E., & Eyal, C. H. (1981). *Media agenda-setting in a presidential election: Issues, images and interest* (T. Takeshita, Trans.). New York: Praeger; in Japanese, Tokyo: Keiso-Shabo.

Weaver, D. H., McCombs, M. E., & Spellman, C. (1975). Watergate and the media: A case study of agenda-setting. *American Politics Quarterly, 3*, 458-472.

Weaver, D. H., Zhu, J., & Willnat, L. (1992). The bridging function of interpersonal communication in agenda-setting. *Journalism Quarterly, 69*(4), 856-867.

Weber, R. E., & Shaffer, W. R. (1972). Public opinion and American state policy-making. *Midwest Journal of Political Science, 16*, 683-699.

Weimann, G. (1994). The influentials as leaders and agenda-setters. In G. Weimann, *The influentials: People who influence people.* Albany: State University of New York Press.

Weisman, A. P. (1986, October). I was a drug-hype junkie. *New Republic,* pp. 14-17.

Weiss, H. (1992). Public issues and argumentation structures: An approach to the study of the contents of media agenda-setting. In S. A. Deetz (Ed.), *Communication yearbook 15* (pp. 374-396). Newbury Park, CA: Sage.

Westley, B. H. (1976). Setting the public agenda: What makes a change? *Journal of Communication, 26*, 43-47.

Wetterer, J. A., & Danowski, J. A. (1992, February). *A network analysis approach to agenda-setting research: The acid rain issue from 1977-1989.* Paper presented at the International Sunbelt Social Networks Conference, San Diego.

Whitney, D. C. (1991). Agenda-setting: Power and contingency. In J. A. Anderson (Ed.), *Communication yearbook 14* (pp. 347-356). Newbury Park, CA: Sage.

Whitney, D. C. (1992, August). *Public, media and policy agenda-setting: Elaborating a model.* Paper presented at the International Association for Mass Communication Research, Guaruja, Brazil.

127

Wilke, J. (1994, June). *Agenda setting in an historical perspective: The coverage of the American Revolution in the German press (1773-1783)*. Paper presented at the International Communication Association, Sydney.

Williams, W., Jr., & Larsen, D. C. (1977). Agenda-setting in an off-election year. *Journalism Quarterly, 54*, 744-749.

Williams, W., Jr., & Semlak, W. D. (1978a). Structural effects of TV coverage on political agenda. *Journal of Communication, 28*(4), 114-119.

Williams, W., Jr., & Semlak, W. D. (1978b). Campaign '76: Agenda setting during the New Hampshire primary. *Journal of Broadcasting and Media Studies, 22*, 531-540.

Williams, W., Jr., Shapiro, M., & Cutbirth, C. (1983). The impact of campaign agendas on perception of issues in 1980 campaign. *Journalism Quarterly, 60*, 226-231.

Willnat, L. (1993, August). *Media priming in the 1992 election campaign: The effects of newspaper stories on evaluations of President Bush*. Paper presented at the Association for Education in Journalism and Mass Communication, Kansas City.

Wilson, J. B., Linz, D., Donnerstein, E., & Stipp, H. (1992). The impact of social issue television programming on attitudes toward rape. *Human Communication Research, 19*(2), 179-208.

Wilson, J. E., & Griswald, W. F. (1993, August). *A test of the interdependence model of agenda-setting within a senatorial election*. Paper presented at the Association for Education in Journalism and Mass Communication, Kansas City.

Wilson, R. (1981). Media coverage of Canadian election campaigns: Horse-race journalism and the meta-campaign. *Journal of Canadian Studies, 15*, 56-68.

Winter, J. P. (1981). Contingent conditions in the agenda-setting process. *Mass communication review yearbook 2* (pp. 235-243). Beverly Hills, CA: Sage.

Winter, J. P., & Eyal, C. (1981). Agenda-setting for the civil rights issue. *Public Opinion Quarterly, 45*, 376-383.

Winter, J. P., Eyal, C., & Rogers, A. H. (1982). Issue-specific agenda-setting: The whole as less than the sum of parts. *Canadian Journal of Communication, 8*, 1-10.

Woodward, J. L. (1934). Qualitative newspaper analysis as a technique of opinion research. *Social Forum, 12*, 526-537.

Wright, C. R. (1986). *Mass communication: A sociological perspective*. New York: Random House.

Yagade, A., & Dozier, D. M. (1990). The media agenda-setting effects of concrete versus abstract issues. *Journalism Quarterly, 67*(1), 3-10.

Yan, J., Jiang, Y., Watt, J. H., Zhu, J., & Snyder, L. B. (1992). *A comparison of four agenda-setting models* (Working paper). Storrs: University of Connecticut, Department of Communication Science.

Young, J., Borgida, E., Sullivan, J., & Aldrich, J. (1987). Personal agendas and the relationship between self-interest and voting behavior. *Social Psychology Quarterly, 50*(1), 64-71.

Zhu, J. (1992a). Issue competition and attention distraction in agenda-setting: A zero-sum perspective. *Journalism Quarterly, 69*(4), 825-836.

Zhu, J. (1992b). *Media agenda-setting and priming during the deficit crisis and the Gulf War: A time-series analysis*. Unpublished paper, University of Connecticut, Storrs, Department of Communication Science.

Zhu, J. (in press). Media agenda-setting theory: Telling what the public think about. In D. P. Cushman & B. Kovacic (Eds.), *Watershed research traditions in human communication theory*. Albany: State University of New York Press.

128

Zhu, J., Watt, J. H., Snyder, L. B., Yan, J., & Jiang, Y. (1993). Public issue priority formation: Media agenda-setting and social interaction. *Journal of Communication, 43*(1), 8-29.

Zimmerman, W. (1973). Issue area and foreign-policy process: A research note in search of a general theory. *American Political Science Review, 67*(2), 1204-1212.

Zucker, H. G. (1978). The variable nature of news media influence. In B. D. Ruben (Ed.), *Communication yearbook 2* (pp. 235-246). New Brunswick, NJ: Transaction.

Author Index

Ader, C. R., 18, 28, 68, 91
Al-Haqeel, A.S., 98
Anokwa, K., 98
Ansolabehere, S., 3
Asp, K., 98

Ball-Rokeach, 16
Baseheart, J. R., 51, 52
Baumgartner, F. R., 55, 72, 75, 79, 88, 89, 95
Becker, L. B., 51
Blumer, H., 15, 17, 55, 60, 67, 71, 75
Boorstin, D., 43
Boot, W., 69, 70
Borre, O., 98
Bosk, C. L., 3, 67, 98
Bosso, C. J., 75
Brecher, M., 79
Bregman, D., 45
Brewer, J., 99
Brooks, S. C., 80
Brosius, H., 50, 66, 90, 98
Burd, G., 93
Byrnes, J. E., 51
Carragee, K., 14, 17
Chaffee, S. H., 24, 48, 98
Chang, S., 15, 33, 34, 35, 36, 57, 57, 58, 68, 91
Cherry, D., 94
Clarke, F., 51
Clemmer, C. L., 51
Cobb, R. W., 2, 3, 9, 78, 79
Cohen, B. C., 1, 9, 10, 12, 45, 67, 76, 100
Cohen, M., 74, 77
Cook, F. L., 93, 99

Cook, T. D., 99
Crigler, A. N., 5, 33, 55

Danielian, L., 19
Danielson, W., 15
Davis, F. J., 7
Dearing, J. W., 5, 15, 33, 35, 36, 45, 51, 55, 56, 57, 58, 59, 68, 75, 91
DeFleur, M. L., 15
DeGeorge, W. F., 35, 68
Derksen, L., 75, 97
Deutschmann, P. J., 15
Doppelt, J. C., 93, 99
Downs, A., 55, 61, 66, 71, 75, 82, 90

Eichhorn, W., 64
Einsiedel, E. F., 51
Elder, C. D., 2, 3, 9, 78, 79
Entman, R. M., 64
Erbring, L., 53, 93, 94
Erikson, R. S., 73, 92
Ettema, J. S., 93, 99
Eyal, C. H., 13, 35, 48, 68, 98

Finnegan, J. R., Jr., 3, 67
Fiske, S., 63
Fitzgerald, F., 30
Funkhouser, G. R., 9, 18, 40, 41, 42, 43, 44, 47, 48, 49, 91

Gadir, S., 98
Gamson, W. A., 15, 17, 55
Gans, H. J., 17

129

Subject Index

Advertising, role in agenda-setting, 28, 98

Agendas:
   defined, 2
   measuring, 17-22, 35-39, 45-49, 64-65, 66-67, 68, 83-84
   Agendas and Instability in America Politics (Baumgartner & Jones), 55

Agenda-setting:
   as political process, 1-5, 5 (figure)
   comparisons of approaches to, 89-90
   data disaggregation in research on, 54-55, 88-90, 92-95
   defined, 1-2
   future study questions for, 95-98
   generalizations about, 90-92
   history of research on, 8-13, 9 (table) , 10 (table)
   in Germany, 50, 64, 98
   in Japan, 37, 48-49, 54 (n5)
   international issues and, 69-70, 78-79, 95, 98
   longitudinal vs. hierarchy studies, 40-41, 54-55, 88-90
   multimethod research for, 99
   private vs. public process of, 95-96
   time sequences in, 67-70, 68 (figure), 71 (n4)
   See also Media agendas; Policy agendas; Public agendas

AIDS, media agenda on, 15, 30-31, 32-33, 56-60, 57 (figure), 82-83, 83 (figure), 91-92

Alternative specification, 74

Audiences:

active vs. passive roles of, 55
issue displacement by, 66-67, 95
psychological processes of, 54-55, 60-61, 62-65
rejection of media agenda by, 5, 52-53
threshold of attention, 11-12, 64-65, 65 (figure)
variables affecting, 46-47, 50-53, 54 (n7)
See also Media; Public agendas

Bandwagon effects, 15, 89
Behavior changes, 82-83, 83 (figure), 97
Bias, Len, 19, 20-21, 29
Blacks, issue salience and, 47, 94
Brazilian famine, 69-70

Celebrities. *See* AIDS
Chapel Hill (N. C.) study, 6-7, 12-13, 23 (n2), 41-42, 48, 50, 67, 93
   comparisons with Funkhouser's study, 44-45, 45 (table)
Charlotte Observer, 73
Cigarettes. *See* Smoking
Citizen advocacy, 31
Civil rights issues, in public agenda, 46
Conflicts, development of issues from, 2-3
Congress, U. S., 25
   policy agenda measurements through, 18, 84-86, 85 (figure)
Content analysis, 18, 35-39, 83

About the Authors

James W. Dearing is Associate Professor of Communication and Interim Director of Doctoral Studies in the Department of Communication at Michigan State University. He received a PhD in Communication Theory and Research from the Annenberg School for Communication at the University of Southern California in 1989, and teaches courses about social change models, research design, program evaluation, mass communication theory, and information technology in organizations. Dearing has been principal investigator for research sponsored by the U.S. National Science Foundation, the U.S. Environmental Protection Agency, and the U.S. Agency for Health Care Policy and Research. In 1994, he was Visiting Assistant Professor at the University of Michigan, and was awarded the Thomas J. Kiresuk Award for Excellence in Scientific Research by the U.S. Knowledge Utilization Society. He is the author of four books, including *Growing a Japanese Science City: Communication in Scientific Research* (1995).

Dr. Everett M. Rogers is Professor and Chair, Department of Communication and Journalism at the University of New Mexico. He taught at Iowa State, Ohio State, Michigan State, the University of Michigan, Stanford, and the University of Southern California, enroute to Albuquerque. Rogers is known for his book, *Diffusion of Innovations*, recently published in its fourth edition. With James Dearing, Rogers has been studing the agenda-setting process for AIDS and other issues since 1987.